PRAISE FOR
BUILD YOUR OWN EARTH OVEN

This new edition is a clear and concise manual on building a fun, people and earth friendly oven that…will bake your bread and all incredibly well…. [it] covers all the details with insight and inspiration [and] guides you gently towards a well-spring of creativity within, to manifest a hands-on wholesomeness without.
— Alan Scott, master oven-builder and coauthor (with Dan Wing) of
The Bread Builders, Hearth Loaves and Masonry Ovens

…not only great for making ovens and bread, but also the best introduction to building with earth. …all you need to know about materials and processes; makes it simple, quick, and easy.
— Charmaine Taylor, Taylor Publishing, California

…The illustrations really make it accessible, and the information is such a good blend of science and love.
— Marc K., Japan

Your drawings and diagrams are warm and practical and they match your helpful, unassuming, flexible voice…. The prospect of making an oven seems less intimidating because you give so many options, directions, and encouragements.
— Carrie M., Utah

I am loving [your book], just totally loving it…. I appreciate your energy to do this for all us mud/oven/bread/artist people. I applaud you for your work. Thank you.
— Judy S., AZ

Your book is an excellent guide to building an Earthen Oven and lots more…. My son-in-law just finished an Italian bread and pizza oven [that] cost $4,000. I told him I will soon build a horno of adobe for less than $100.
— Clint T., CO

Thank You! Thank You! The permaculture students love your book — our best-seller!
— Emily, "WE DESIGN," SEATTLE

I'm an ardent breadbaker and I think your book is inspiring, comprehensive, and very practical…. it is beautiful!
— Monika G., California

Two students and I built an oven for our school auction. We tested it at a gala house warming party: all the guests abandoned the catered food and began devouring plain simple bread and butter…. People were in fresh baked bread euphoria — a success!
—Warren C., 3d grade teacher, Washington

I love how you have made function into art with your ovens…..
— Olivia L., Utah

8 SIMPLE STEPS TO...

DIG DIRT! (P. 20)

LAY A FOUNDATION (P. 25)

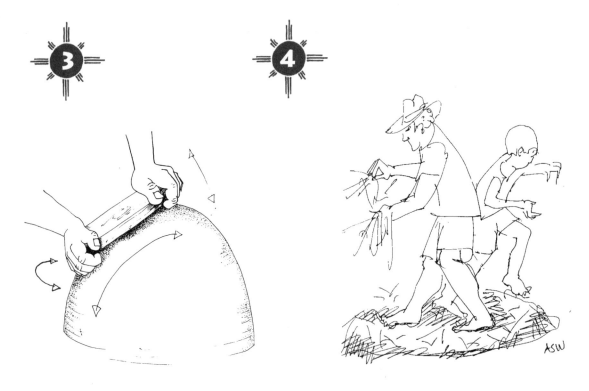

MAKE A SAND FORM (P. 29)

MIX MUD (P. 32)

A BASIC MUD OVEN

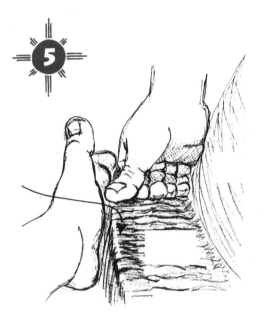

BUILD UP LAYERS (P.34)

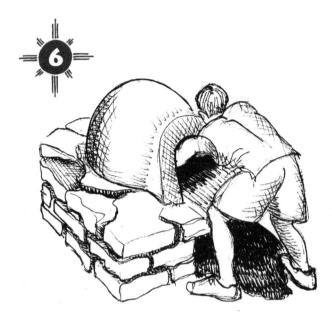

REMOVE SAND FORM (P. 37)

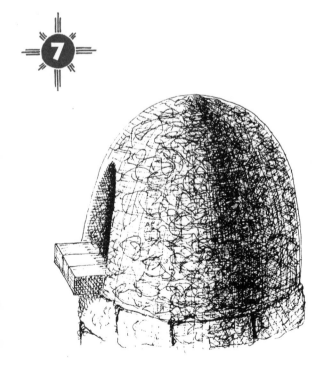

SCULPT & FINISH (P. 38)

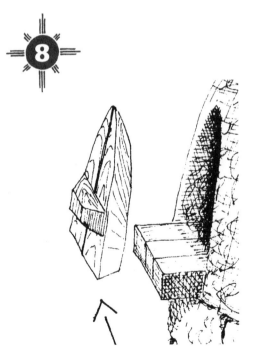

MAKE A DOOR (P. 41)

A BASIC MUD OVEN ON AN "URBANITE" FOUNDATION

This oven was built in a workshop for members of a local guild of potters and ceramic artists. It was done in a day, from foundation hole to finish plaster! The tools leaning against the oven are used for cleaning the oven prior to baking, and are called a "rooker" and "scuffle." (The concrete chunks ("urbanite") for the foundation were salvaged from the city public works department. They pile them up in a field by the dumptruck load, and are happy for folks to come take them away.)

BUILD YOUR OWN
EARTH OVEN

A LOW-COST, WOOD-FIRED MUD OVEN, SIMPLE SOURDOUGH BREAD, PERFECT LOAVES

FOR BAKERS &
BEGINNERS
BOTH

KIKO DENZER

Build Your Own Earth Oven:
A Low-Cost, Wood-Fired Mud Oven,
Simple Sourdough Bread, Perfect Loaves
Second edition, copyright 2000 by Kiko Denzer;
all rights reserved; For permission, contact the publisher.
fifth printing, 2004

Illustrations and photos by the author, except as noted;
drawings on pages 21, 36, 50, 62, courtesy of
Ann Wiseman and Ansayre Press.
"Sourdough Haiku" on page 52
courtesy of the author.

Distributed to the book trade by
Chelsea Green Publishing
White River Junction, Vermont
(800) 639-4099; www.chelseagreen.com

TO ORDER BOOKS:
See special re-order coupon on back page, or contact us!

Hand Print Press,
Post Office Box 576
Blodgett, OR, 97326, USA
handiko@cmug.com

OTHER TITLES FROM HAND PRINT PRESS:
Put your hands in the dirt:
Art Made With Mud, Kids, & Communities
by Kiko Denzer; "art is what we do," and this
book focuses on simple earthen murals & sculpture to
more complex things like labyrinths and sundials.

Making Things: A Handbook of Creative Discovery
By Ann Wiseman; a great hands-on curriculum
for learning-by-doing, this is a classic collection of
wonderfully illustrated instructions for 125 projects
involving just minimal tools and household materials.
Forthcoming in 2004.

Publisher's Cataloging-in-Publication Data
Denzer, Kiko
Build Your Own Earth Oven:
A Low-Cost, Wood-Fired Mud Oven,
Simple Sourdough Bread, Perfect Loaves / Kiko Denzer. 2nd ed.
119 p. : ill; 25 cm.
Library of Congress Card Catalogue Number: 01-101050.
ISBN 0-9679846-0-2
    1. Stoves
    2. Earth Construction
    3. Cookery (Bread)
    4. Bread
TX 657.057 d4 2001
641.58 Denzer

Talking is teaching.
Listening is learning.
Education is sharing.
Experience is a seed,
and even the bitterest seed will grow.
Culture is the fruit of common experience —
a common responsibility, and
our common wealth.
If work is love made visible,
then love is everywhere you look.

YOUR OVEN STORIES

For this fourth printing, at the very end of the book, I have filled up some blank pages with a gallery of stories and pictures sent in by readers and oven friends willing to share and celebrate their experiences. It has been remarkable to see and hear how a simple thing like an oven can create new space, new relationships, and new ways of doing things — and not only cooking! (Some of the stories are from people who offer workshops on oven building, as well as other more environmental, and/or traditional ways of doing things. Contact info, where appropriate, is included.)

    If you'd like to share an oven story, perhaps in a future edition or on a website (volunteer host needed!), please contact me at Hand Print Press, POB 576, Blodgett, OR, 97326, (handiko@cmug.com). If you'd like to order a copy of this book, there's a discount coupon on the last page. And finally, thank you to those who asked and answered, and those who continue to build, learn, bake, eat, and celebrate!

— *Kiko Denzer*, November, 2002

ORDER OF THE OVEN

"…Your book set off a cascade of events in my life, starting with the gathering of materials, planning and replanning, daubing mud and plaster and baking bread and pizzas. Now I'm a disciple of the Order of The Wood-Fired Oven. Friends and family scatter when they see me, because they know that's all that I want to talk about!"

— Ron Henderson, Turner, OR

SQUEALS OF DELIGHT

"…The oven has become a focal point when friends come to visit…I fire it up and let the bread rise, and we sit in the shade of a nearby tree so we can smell it baking. We've learned to savor the process…

    ….I built it outside of a miniature village in my backyard. My whole family joined in…The village has five buildings, and while my grandkids enjoy them, they never felt much kinship…because I did it for them (even though they helped…). But mixing the cob while getting deliriously muddy, and hearing squeals of delight while stomping in some more…it's a sound that touches the soul…."

— Greg Jones, Eugene, OR

MAYA AT INTABA'S

A commercial earthen oven, at Intaba's Kitchen, a gourmet organic restaurant in Corvallis, Oregon, built by the author. The whole place is a celebration of earth, and not just because the excellent food comes from sun and soil: a 140' cob wall wraps the courtyard in a warm embrace; sculpted benches (one of them heated from within by radiant hot water pipes) make nooks for shared meals; there's an earthen mural on the porch wall, and earthen bas-relief decorative detailing in the dining room.

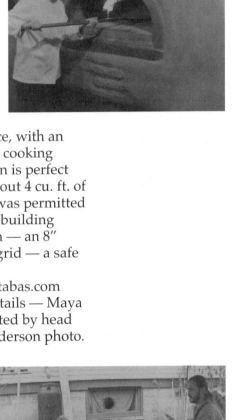

The oven is made with grog (crushed firebrick), instead of sand, to minimize thermal shock; the hearth floor is 4x4 feet, with 12 inches of thermal mass, 12 inches of pumice insulation, and 2 inches of mud plaster; total diameter about 9 feet; a *big*, basic mud oven. The refractory cement doorframe was cast in place, with an exterior surround of regular cement stucco. After cooking pizza all day, and with no additional fire, the oven is perfect for bread in the morning. Fuel consumption is about 4 cu. ft. of fuel/day (two large rectangular plastic tubs). It was permitted as a "cast clay-sand refractory oven;" though the building department did ask for an engineered foundation — an 8" thick concrete table, with half inch rebar on a 6" grid — a safe cave in event of earthquake.

For menu, photos, and more, see www.intabas.com (click on "Maya's homepage" for construction details — Maya is the Hindu Goddess of creation; a name suggested by head baker Kirsten Schumacher (in photo)). Ocean Anderson photo.

FERTILE GROUND

The Fertile Ground Guesthouse, in Olympia, Washington, offers green lodging for business and family travelers. They decided they needed an oven, and asked Elliot Ridgway to lead the project (on the left, tossing a mud ball – low tech material transport – fun and energy efficient). The Guesthouse, if you're visiting, is at 311 9th Av. SE, Olympia, WA 98501; 360/352-2428; www.fertileground.org. K. Nelson photo.

oven stories continued on page 128

TABLE OF CONTENTS

PREFACE

Mud — earth, clay, the stuff under your feet — is a near perfect building material. Thousands of years ago, the first oven was made of mud. People all over the world still bake in earthen ovens, and the best ovens in the fanciest bakeries are often brick — which, after all, is made of kiln-fired mud.

If you're a beginner, remember: even if you've never built a thing, your hands will show you how if you'll just start. We are all born into the tradition of building and making — it's how we learn to tie shoes, cook eggs, swing a hammer, drive a car, and even how to play video games or surf the web (technology still begins, and usually ends, with our hands).

Building a mud oven isn't complicated. Pay more attention to what you're doing than to what I've written. Common sense and experience will be your best teachers. If you're uncomfortable or feeling inexperienced, go slow. Take a break if you don't know what to do next. Solutions will come, and they will come easiest if you aren't in a hurry.

Granted, a good oven alone doesn't make good bread, which is why this book includes a simple introduction to sourdough. But a mud oven (with help from the baker) can produce perfect bread — equal or superior to the fanciest $5 loaf. I once took ten loaves of mud-baked bread to a wedding party for a German friend — five sourdough rye, and five sourdough wheat. All his German family and friends said, "this is just like home!" and asked where they could buy it. Some of them begged for a loaf to sustain them as they traveled in a land not known for its bread. I later made a portable oven (of lightweight pumice — on a four by eight foot trailer) to provide pizza for a local summer festival. My wife Hannah was head baker and a caterer friend provided dough and toppings; they made and sold about 250 pizzas per day, each one cooked to perfection in two to three minutes. People raved.

A mud oven is also a good place to make mistakes: under-cooked lumps, and burnt or sandy crusts. But under-cooked dough can lead to grand discoveries: I sliced, toasted, and crushed up some under-cooked bread once because I was loathe to throw away good (almost) raw material. I put the granules in jars on my shelves. One breadless morning, I decided to try soaking the stuff in milk with a little sugar — and heard echoes of Euell Gibbons praising the flavor of "wild hickory nuts." Now I always keep some on hand, even when I don't under-cook the bread. As for burning bread, I have learned that "burnt" is a matter of opinion. In some European countries, crusts that others might consider burnt are prized for the more intense flavor of the dark crust. And while charred is charred the world over, you can always cut away the burnt bits. Once, as an experiment (and because it was ready to bake and still rising fast), Hannah cooked a loaf in a 700 degree pizza oven. In less than ten minutes, the bread came out black, but we pared off the crust, and found it perfect inside. And of course, sometimes when you bake in a mud oven you get sandy grit in your crusts. Materials vary, and while most of them will work, some work better than others. When I get sandy bread, I just trim the crusts, bake in pans or on paper, or build a better oven.

Making things means making the most of your mistakes. There are also, of course, risks and responsibilities. Oven fires are well-contained, and pretty safe, but you can't be too careful! Watch your fire, but also build so that an un-watched fire can't spread to timber, grasslands, buildings, etc. Where I live, there's no fire department, and I don't have fire insurance. I have to be careful, and have tried to convey prudence and caution in what I write. However, you may want to check your plans against local fire and/or building codes and make sure that what and how you build won't compromise your insurance policies. For more comprehensive technical or safety information, you could start with titles in the Resources section.

Good building and baking to you! Please do let me know if you have questions or suggestions (or photos!) that might help to improve a future edition.

Kiko Denzer

RESOURCES
Recommended books and additional useful information is mentioned in side-bars like this. More complete information can be found in the Resources *section on page 112.*

A BASIC MUD OVEN IN THE TEMPERATE RAINFOREST OF OREGON
…Built by Ianto Evans, who has designed and built earthen stoves for years, and from whom I first learned about mud ovens. He and a team of cobbers also built the "cob cottage" next to it. The oven is finished with a traditional African plaster called litema *("dee-TAY-ma"), made of cow manure and colored clay.*

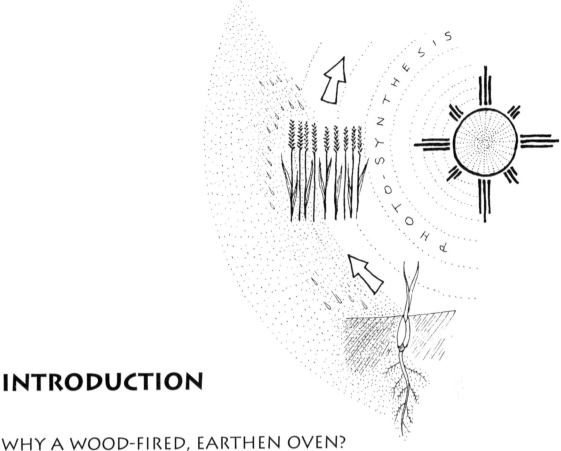

INTRODUCTION

WHY A WOOD-FIRED, EARTHEN OVEN?

Modern cookbooks make bread-baking seem complicated and difficult — which it is not. Building and baking in a wood-fired earthen oven restores the simplicity of bread by returning you to essentials: earth, water, air, and fire.

Plants transform the energy of the sun into woody material, fire transforms wood into energy, and the massive walls of an earthen oven absorb and concentrate that energy as heat. After a couple of hours, the oven is hot enough that you can remove the fire and bake bread. The hot, dense mud radiates its stored heat at a steady rate (like the sun!)

Radiant heat is fundamental to our very existence — from it we have photosynthesis and weather, food and shelter, and sunny days on the beach, not to mention wheat and bread. The architect Christopher Alexander says that humans have a biologically built-in human preference for radiant heat — his answer to why people prefer an open fireplace to an open heating vent. Perhaps that's another reason why bread is better baked in a wood-fired oven....

Radiation is one of three ways that heat can be transferred from oven to bread: the other two are convection and conduction. Convection is the reason why warm air rises —

heated air molecules move faster — the faster they move, the farther apart they get and the fewer of them there are in a given amount of space. Fewer molecules have less weight, making hot air lighter than cold air; thus, hot air rises. Convection works in any gas or liquid, but it doesn't work in solid materials, like brick or metal. So heat doesn't always rise, or at least, not exclusively. In a solid material, heat moves in all directions, by a method called conduction. Conduction is how a hot frying pan cooks an egg — direct contact with hot metal transfers heat very quickly to the egg, which cooks much faster than it would if it was only in contact with hot air.

Modern ovens depend primarily on convection, so it's not the oven that does the cooking; instead, the air carries the heat to your bread, and the bread cooks. Even if a modern oven has no hot or cold spots, baking more than two loaves requires careful arrangement so the air can carry equal amounts of heat to every loaf. Fancy, so-called "convection" ovens try to improve the situation with a fan that hurries the hot air around. Special baking pans or stones can help improve your bread, but they are poor substitutes for the original oven, which was made of earth.

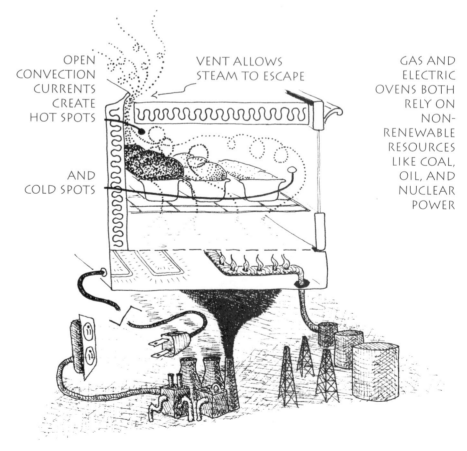

OPEN CONVECTION CURRENTS CREATE HOT SPOTS

AND COLD SPOTS

VENT ALLOWS STEAM TO ESCAPE

GAS AND ELECTRIC OVENS BOTH RELY ON NON-RENEWABLE RESOURCES LIKE COAL, OIL, AND NUCLEAR POWER

BUILD YOUR OWN EARTH OVEN

An earthen oven bakes your bread using all three kinds of heat transfer: radiant heat from the hot walls; conducted heat from hot bricks through the bottom of the loaf, and convected heat from hot, steamy air swirling inside the sealed oven. With all this heat from every direction, many loaves cook as easily as one. In addition, the different kinds of heat working together improve what is called "oven spring" — the irregular air holes and high loaf that happen when a vigorous batch of yeasty dough gives a final surge of activity in response to a hot floor and hot, steamy air. In addition, superheated steam caramelizes the sugars in the outside layer of dough, producing a lovely, crisp, substantial crust.

Building and baking with a wood-fired earthen oven not only makes wonderful bread, it can also teach you things you'll never learn with a modern oven, bread machine, or book. Instead of turning switches, you will come to know earth, air, fire and water, and you will come to know the life they give to grain and yeast and bread, as well as the life they give to us. Books can explain why, but the best way to really understand is to do it yourself. "You got to go there to know there."

RESOURCE: The Bread Builders, *by Dan Wing and Alan Scott, is a wonderful and complete reference on the science and art of baking in retained heat ovens. It explains in detail the specifics of recent research into yeasts, bacteria, and the fermentation of dough, and puts it all into context with visits to well-known professional bakers. It also includes plans for building a professional-quality brick oven and instructions for using it. If you want to graduate from mud to brick and open your own bakery, or if you just want to know more about bread and ovens, this is an essential book*

EARTHEN OVENS ARE BETTER FOR BAKING BECAUSE THEY PROVIDE AN EVEN SOURCE OF ALL THREE KINDS OF HEAT:
1. *Radiant heat, from hot, massive walls*
2, *Conducted heat, from direct contact with a hot brick floor*
3. *Convected heat, from hot, moving (& steam-charged) air.*

EARTHEN BUILDING, OR WHAT IS "COB," ANYWAY?

Earth is the most common, and perhaps the most versatile building material on the planet. Mixed with sand and straw, a clay subsoil will become very hard and durable; indeed, it was the first, natural "concrete." In the Americas, this material is called "adobe," from an Arabic word, al-toba, meaning "the brick." Invading Moors brought the word to Spain from North Africa, where the ancient tradition of mud building continues today. In Britain, the continuing tradition of earthen building is called cob, from an old English word meaning "lump." The Brits skipped the step of forming bricks, and made their walls by packing wet blobs of mud on top of each other, letting them dry, and carving them smooth. Five-hundred-year-old cob houses are common in Devon, England, where they are recognized on historic registers, and command high prices when sold.

Protected by roof and foundation from direct rain and snow, earthen buildings hold up very well, even in damp, windy Devon. I built a mud studio in the temperate rainforest of the Oregon coast range, and it is warmer and drier than my wooden cabin — not to mention that it's impervious to fire, and the bugs that eat wood can't stomach it.

Building a mud oven is like building a mud house, on a smaller scale. The dome shape is basic in nature, common to beehives, bird's nests, caves, cliff dwellings, igloos, huts, and the Houston Astrodome — strong, self-supporting, easy to build and heat.

MUD MAN OVEN & REAR VIEW, OREGON, 1995

In rainy climates like the Pacific Northwest, ovens are best sheltered under a deep eave like this, or under a freestanding roof. Protection from wind-driven rain is more important for the baker than for the oven, which would only "melt" if it was completely submerged. Ovens can also be built indoors. Take every possible precaution against accidental spread of fire, just as you would with a fireplace. Yes, it's the same cob cottage as the picture on page four. The oven door is under the fish chimney, at the rear.

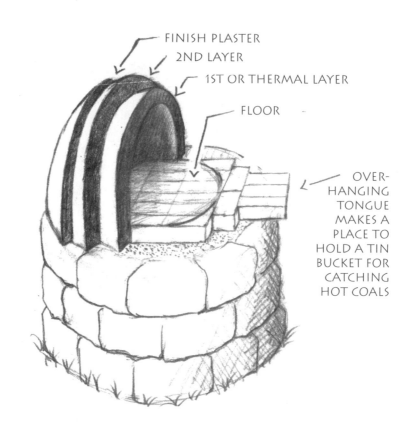

FINISH PLASTER

2ND LAYER

1ST OR THERMAL LAYER

FLOOR

OVER-
HANGING
TONGUE
MAKES A
PLACE TO
HOLD A TIN
BUCKET FOR
CATCHING
HOT COALS

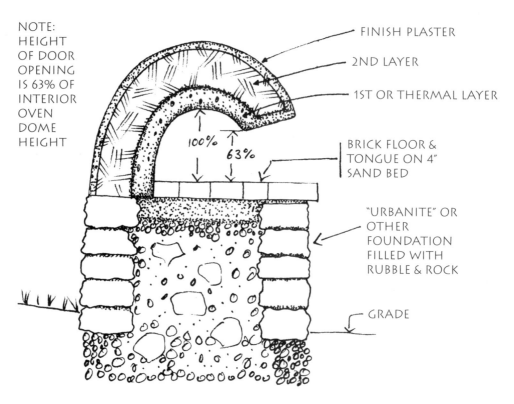

NOTE:
HEIGHT
OF DOOR
OPENING
IS 63% OF
INTERIOR
OVEN
DOME
HEIGHT

FINISH PLASTER

2ND LAYER

1ST OR THERMAL LAYER

100%

63%

BRICK FLOOR &
TONGUE ON 4"
SAND BED

"URBANITE" OR
OTHER
FOUNDATION
FILLED WITH
RUBBLE & ROCK

GRADE

BUILD YOUR OWN EARTH OVEN

CHAPTER ONE: BUILD A BASIC MUD OVEN

The basic oven is a simple, dome-shaped shell of mud and sand. It can be one or more layers thick. In order to provide as much useful information as possible, this chapter talks about how to build a three-layer oven with no insulation. If you want to try a simpler one layer oven, or a more complicated, insulated oven, see Chapter Five.

The diagrams show the layers as follows:

1. A dense thermal layer (approx. three inches), with no straw.
2. A less dense layer with added straw (up to six inches). This is where you can do rough sculpting; the extra mass will also hold more heat, which means more baking time from a single firing. (If you decide to insulate, this would be the insulation layer.)
3. A finish layer, or "plaster," of one to two inches.

Note that the diagram shows a 27 inch oven, which refers to a 27 inch diameter baking floor. The total diameter, however, is about 48 inches, or four feet, because each layer adds twice its thickness to the overall dimension.

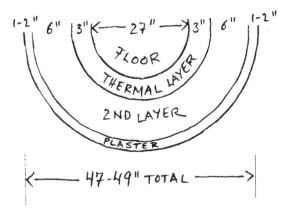

HOW BIG AN OVEN SHOULD I MAKE?

Although the plans show a 27 inch oven, you may want to make a smaller or larger one. In order to determine an optimum size, decide how much and what kind of baking you'll want to do in it. Will you be baking daily? Weekly? Monthly? Twice a summer? Just breads? Or meat too? Turkey, roasts, etc., may need a larger, higher door, which means a larger oven overall, and/or a brick or metal door frame.

If you only bake a couple of loaves at a time, you'll quickly get frustrated with a huge oven that requires lots of wood to heat. A twenty-seven inch oven is pretty sizable. Three feet is big. Especially if your fuel supply is limited, you may want to limit oven size accordingly. A friend's youngest daughter asked if she could make a tiny one, 8-12 inches in diameter, just big enough to bake a few cookies — why not?!

To figure your size requirements, lay out loaf pans, baking trays, or rounds of paper as big as you make your loaves, and see how big a circle you need to contain it all. That's how big an oven you should make. (Remember that loaves rise and/or spread, and that the wider your door (to accommodate cookie sheets or pizza, for example) the more heat your oven will lose.)

GETTING ORGANIZED
LOCATE YOUR OVEN SITE

If you take the time to answer the following questions (on paper or in discussion), you can avoid some real headaches.
- Where do you prepare your bread and other foods?
- Where is most convenient to your kitchen?
- Is the ground roughly level?
- Will you use the oven when it's cold, dark, or rainy?
- Can the oven and any necessary pathways be well-lit at night?
- Are there any spots already protected by a roof or overhang?
- Which way does the wind blow? Where will smoke go?
- Can you site the oven so the door faces away from prevailing winds?
- What are the fire hazards?
- Where do you store your fire wood? Is it convenient to the oven site? Might your wood shed (safely) serve as oven shed, or vice-versa?
- Do you need to have your plans approved for compliance with the building code, or to protect against possibly voiding fire insurance?

WHEN LOCATING YOUR OVEN, THINK ABOUT:

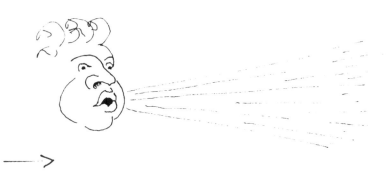

FIRE WILL
BURN EASIER
WITH DOOR
FACING AWAY
FROM WIND ——>

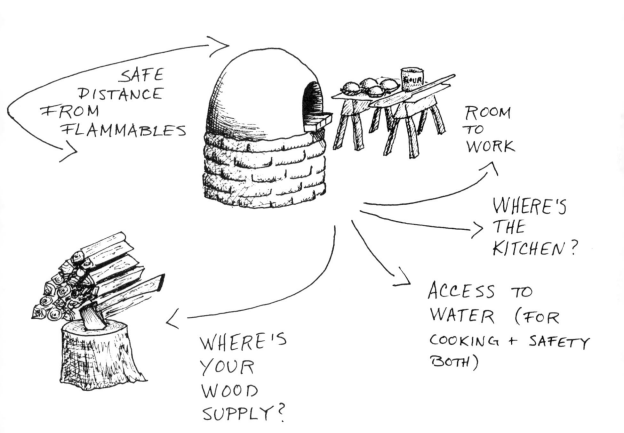

SAFE
DISTANCE
FROM
FLAMMABLES

ROOM
TO
WORK

WHERE'S
THE
KITCHEN?

ACCESS TO
WATER (FOR
COOKING + SAFETY
BOTH)

WHERE'S
YOUR
WOOD
SUPPLY?

MATERIALS & TOOLS

In this consumer culture, it is immensely satisfying to make something beautiful and useful with just what you have on hand! So before you buy a lot of stuff, look around home and yard (or your neighbor's, or the dump or dumpsters) to see what might suit your purpose.

Amounts listed are estimates, and this isn't a cookbook. Every site, every combination of materials, and every oven is different — amounts will vary accordingly. Collect more than you think you'll need — it's easier to use or get rid of a little sand than it is to stop in the middle of a project to get more. If you're having trouble finding what you need, look at Chapter four for ideas on how to make do with what you've got.

The chart "on weight and volume" is not exact; materials vary in weight and volume according to what they are and how much water they contain; wheelbarrows and buckets vary in size; backs and arms vary in carrying capacity. My barrow is one of the six cubic foot variety. Yours may be smaller or bigger. A cubic foot is about seven and a half gallons. Sand and soil are heavy, but easy to move in smaller amounts.

APPROX.

5 GALS = 1 CU. FOOT (12" × 12" × 12") = ± 100 LBS SAND/DIRT
± 40 LBS WATER

= + + = ± 300 LBS OF SAND/DIRT

½ TON = + + = ± 900 LBS SAND/DIRT

ON WEIGHT AND VOLUME

One cubic yard equals 27 cubic feet. One cubic foot is about seven and a half gallons, but a 5 gallon bucket makes a good approximate measuring cup, if you need one; sand or rock generally weighs more than100 pounds per cubic foot. Three five-gallon buckets make a reasonable wheelbarrow load of about 300 pounds (many small loads are easier on your back). A half ton pickup (not overloaded) holds 9-1200 pounds, or a third to a half yard of sand — about three to five wheelbarrow loads.

MATERIALS LIST

- Water: if you don't have easy access to a hose, buckets will do.
- Dirt (subsoil): several buckets to a wheelbarrow full — depending on clay content (see Step One). Save topsoil for your garden.
- Sand to mix with mud: a couple of (large) wheelbarrows full; "sharp" (not rounded or beach) sand is best; ideally the biggest grains should be about 1/8th of an inch — coarser than "mason's" sand. My local gravel pit fills my pickup with "concrete sand" for $5 — free if I shovel it!
- Sand for the oven form: a couple of wheelbarrows full; this can be beach sand, concrete sand, mason's sand, river sand, etc. It should hold its shape when wet.
- Straw: a small, two-string bale is more than enough, and should cost less than $5. Or ask if you can sweep the loose straw out of a horse or cow barn; it takes a lot!
- Foundation: a three foot high base 48 inches in diameter requires about a yard of rock or "urbanite;" but you can build a foundation with less — see Chapter Four.
- Foundation filler: 1/3 to one yard or more of drain rock or rubble, (depending on foundation depth).
- Floor: 21 standard firebricks, 4.5x9 inches each, *or* 28 standard red bricks, 3.75x8 inches. Bricks may be new or used, but should be smooth, flat, and free of chips and old mortar. Prices will vary; red brick is cheaper than fire brick, which costs about $1 each. In general, red brick is fine for less than weekly use. Drawings show firebrick.
- Wood for a baking door: a slab an inch or two thick, approximately 9x14 inches, and nails or screws as needed.
- Newspaper

TOOL LIST

- Shovel
- Wheelbarrow
- Five-gallon plastic buckets
- Tape measure
- Tarps: 6x8 foot min.; a bigger tarp turns a heavy load more easily. Woven plastic lumber wrap (in the dumpster at the lumber yard) is sometimes stronger than blue tarp —free, recyclable "waste." Tyvek or Typar housewrap also works, and scraps are sometimes available at construction sites.)

WHAT'S "URBANITE"? *Also known as busted-up concrete floor or sidewalk slab on its way to the dump, "urbanite" is a great "urban resource" that makes a pretty nice building material. It's cheap, easy to stack and strong. A friend got dumptruck loads delivered free and made it into the foundation of a large cob house. I believe the term was coined by David Eisenberg, an architect who is working to make the International Building Code more environmentally responsible, among other things.*

- spoons, spatulas, dull knives, etc.,
- lumber scraps (1x4; 2x4; etc.)
- old clothes to get dirty in, and boots if you don't want to go barefoot
- hardware cloth (optional), (1/4 or 1/2 inch), on a 2x2 foot or larger wood frame; for screening sand, soil, and straw (see photo on p. 64); expanded metal lath also works, and may be cheaper — just beware sharp edges that grab unsuspecting flesh.
- spirit level, two or four foot (optional)
- machete, hatchet, or weed whacker and large garbage can (optional)
- spray bottle/mister (optional)

FOR INSULATING WITH STRAW-CLAY:
- sheet or two of old plywood, tin roofing, or other hard surface
- hay fork
- electric drill with a paint-mixing attachment

TO MAKE OVEN TOOLS:
- old hoe and/or metal weed "whip" and/or shovel
- wooden stick about four feet long
- clean rags
- 1x6 or 1x8 softwood scrap lumber, three to four feet long, *or* three feet of 1x2 and approx. 4x12 inches of masonite or thin plywood.

WORK SPACE
   You'll need space to mix materials on a tarp — nine by twelve feet minimum, plus plenty of room around the edges for helpers, tools, materials, etc. A cramped space makes more work.

BEAUTY & SCULPTURE

   Earthen building is inherently sculptural, so it's hard to make an ugly oven. What you (and all other sculptors) do is reshape space and define new relationships between where you live and what you do.
   Mud is lovely and easy to work with, and the openings of the oven suggest all manner of real and mythical figures. You can think of it as a totemic structure, a house god, or a piece of abstract art. Even by itself, the basic oven has all the taut, expectant beauty of a pregnant belly!

ON "WATERPROOFING"

An earthen oven, like a living thing, breathes. When baking, it "exhales" steam. Putting a non-breathable, waterproof finish (like cement or paint) on an oven is like putting on a rubber suit to exercise — it traps moisture. Just as you'd get soaked with sweat running in a rubber suit, steam from baking will condense against a non-breathable finish and soak back into the oven. Enough of it can soften your oven, and even cause collapse. At the very least, you'll have to dry it out every time you bake, which takes extra time and fuel.

Cement also cracks, allowing water in faster than it can get out. When the mud gets soft enough, it will leak out with the water. Or water freezes, cracks grow, and your oven erodes. So ovens are best finished with water-*resistant* plasters such as lime-sand or clay-manure mixes. Such plasters are breathable, and are traditionally used on earthen buildings in Africa, Central America and England (see Step Seven, and Chapter Five on "Finish Plasters"). However, even the best breathable plaster will suffer from prolonged soaking in wet weather. The best solution is a roof.

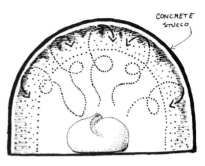

CONCRETE STUCCO

CONCRETE, OR OTHER "WATERPROOF" FINISHES, TRAP WATER VAPOR IN THE OVEN

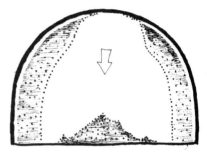

THE RESULTS ARE NOT GOOD

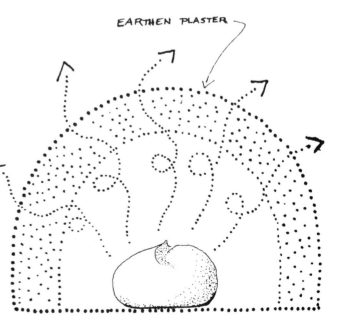

EARTHEN PLASTER

EARTH "BREATHES," WATER VAPOR PASSES THROUGH

A ROOF FOR YOUR OVEN

An outdoor oven without a roof is like — well, an outdoor oven without a roof. It works fine, as long as you have good weather. Traditional southwestern "hornos" seem to survive very well uncovered, but even in a desert environment, a roof will not only protect your oven, it will also create useful work space. You don't need to have it all planned out in advance, however. Build the oven in good weather and try it out. See what you need — a spot to rest a tray, or a big table where you can knead dough and lay out all the pizza makings? When you know, build a structure to suit yourself. The possibilities for roofing an oven could fill another whole book, so I'll just offer a few suggestions and ideas here:

If you just plan for fair-weather baking, a tarp, boards, or an old piece of tin roofing will protect your oven when you're not baking. A simple lean-to or shed roof without walls can be built over the oven on a four-post shed or A-frame. A carport might do, or a long eave on your existing house, or a new shed roof off of an existing building. I built a small temporary oven at home that I wrapped with a couple of sheets of corrugated tin, cut and folded to fit around the door, and nailed to the wood frame — not pretty, but it worked, even for baking in the rain.

CAUTION
Leave generous ventilation gaps (3" min.) between the oven and any-thing that might burn

A TRADITIONAL A-FRAME ROOF FOR A CANADIAN-STYLE OVEN

A SIMPLE FRAME STRUCTURE WITH A SHED ROOF ALSO MAKES ROOM FOR A BREAD SHELF AND TOOLS

BUILD YOUR OWN EARTH OVEN

Consider your oven as the centerpiece for a really beautiful piece of "indigenous" architecture. You could build a semicircular cob enclosure, with a beautiful, living, (and fireproof) sod roof!

AN OVEN CAN TRANSFORM A DEAD CORNER INTO SOCIAL SPACE
An oven can create a new outdoor "room," as shown at this camp. People gather around to watch, help, or just to sit in a beautiful space that previously went unused, even though it was the sunniest spot. Chimney and roof were beautifully crafted by master carpenters at a Natural Building Colloquium.

STEP ONE: DIG!

Soil comes in layers: topsoil is a mix of organic matter (decomposed plants) and inorganic matter (rock, sand, silt, and clay). Below is subsoil, usually a mix of clay, silt, and sand from decomposed rock. Topsoil (especially when it's full of worms, compost, humus, and lots of organic matter), is best for your garden. For building, however, subsoil is better. The ideal mix contains about 15 to 25 percent clay, with the rest silt, sand, and small gravel; it dries into a solid mass that is dense and strong — much like concrete! (Indeed, it *was* the first concrete!)

TOP SOIL: DARK, FULL OF LIFE; OFTEN MORE FERTILE, WITH LESS CLAY

SUBSOIL: COLOR VARIES, LESS PLANT LIFE, OFTEN RICH IN CLAY

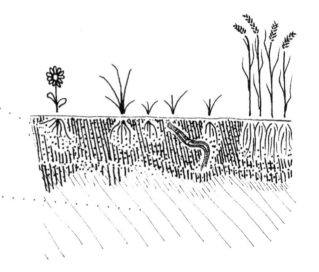

RECOGNIZING CLAY SOIL

Clay subsoil has distinct and recognizable characteristics. It's harder to dig, and doesn't crumble easily. A shovel leaves a shiny cut mark. Add enough water to soften it, and it will roll into snakes between your palms and wrap around your finger with minimal cracking. You can mold it, work it, sculpt it, and when dry, it will be hard and not crumbly. But even when dry and hard, it will still feel slippery because clay particles are flat, and slide across one another smoothly, instead of rolling and grinding. I take a pinch of the stuff in my palm, spit into it, and mix it with a finger. Silt or organic matter feels floury or crumbly. Clay feels sticky, slippery, and a bit greasy.

Having said all that, it's not hard to mistake fine silt for clay. My first big cob project was a wattle and daub woodshed. I was in a hurry, with helpers coming. I'd dug around and found very fine subsoil that looked pretty shiny, sticky, and homogenous. "Clay!" I thought, and didn't both with testing. Nope. It was a light, fine silt that might become clay in a few hundred thousand years. (Though it did work for daub, I don't think it would make a good oven — I should try it one of these days.) Literally forty feet away, however, where the flood plain rises up into the hills around my house, there is beautiful clay soil — so I learned!

You will too; just look around and take your time. If you can't find clay on your site, look at old quarries, riverbanks, ponds, road cuts, building sites, and neighbors' yards. Be careful too. Fill dirt from developed sites or old dumps may be full of broken glass or dangerous debris, and depending on where you dig, you may need to ask permission. (If you absolutely can't find clay soil, see Chapter Four.)

A SHAKE TEST

Most soil is not just dirt, but a mix of different stuff in different sizes. This test separates soil into layers from large to small: sand and gravel first, then silt, and then clay. Pulverize a few handfuls of dry soil to dust; if it's wet, mash it like potatoes, with no lumps! Fill a clear glass jar, half soil, and the rest water; add a teaspoon of salt or liquid soap to help the clay settle faster, and shake hard 'til thoroughly homogenous. Watch: rocks and sand will settle very fast: five to ten seconds for coarse sand; up to 30 minutes for silt; and days or even weeks for clay. IMPORTANT: If the water clears in less than 1/2 hour, you'll know for sure that you don't have enough clay!

SHAKE TEST

— WATER
— CLAY
— SILT (30 MINS.)
— SAND & GRAVEL (40 SECS.)

At 20 or 30 minutes, assuming your water is cloudy with suspended clay, try to locate the point where all the silt has settled. Make a mark there (don't worry if it's hard to tell, you don't need an exact measure — try tapping or gently shaking the jar: whatever is still in solution will vibrate. Make a mark between what moves and what doesn't). You won't be able to tell exactly how much is sand, because wet soil compacts more than dry stuff, but you'll get a rough idea of proportions. In your final cob mix, you want 75-85% sand, and 15-25% clay.

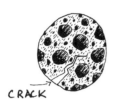

CRACK

SQUISHY MIX
*NO! Too much clay,
the sand grains
don't even touch —
you won't hear
much, and it will
crack as it dries.*

 SAND

 CLAY

CRUNCHY MIX
*YES! Lots of sand,
just enough clay to
stick it together —
you'll be able to
hear the sand grains
crunching against
each other,
shrinkage and
cracking will be
minimal*

PACK MIX
FIRM & HARD

QUICK & DIRTY TEST MIXES

CRUNCH TEST

Sometimes you're lucky and find what cobbers call "redi-mix," a perfect combination of sand and clay. But say you have a soil that looks like it's about half clay. That's too much. If you were to mix it with an equal amount of sand, you'd get one part clay, one part silt or sand (from your soil), and two parts pure sand — roughly one part clay to three parts sand, or 25% clay — just about perfect!

Test different ratios: one part soil to one part sand, one soil to two sand, one to three, one to four, one to five, etc. Keep batches separate so you know which is which. Dampen each mix lightly, like dough for pie crust (moist, sticky, but not a paste), and listen: with a fistful at your ear, you should be able to squeeze and hear sand grinding. If you can't, it probably doesn't have enough sand. Try the next mix.

SNOWBALL TEST

Make a small batch of what you think will be a good mix. Mix it up quite dry (if it's too wet, you'll get confusing results since water alone may hold it together). Pack it into a very firm ball (this can take some minutes to really consolidate it). Drop it on the ground from waist high. It should hold its shape with little or no cracking. If it crumbles into grains and small clumps, it has too little clay. If it goes flat and smooth without cracking at all, it needs sand. If you're not confident yet, learn more:

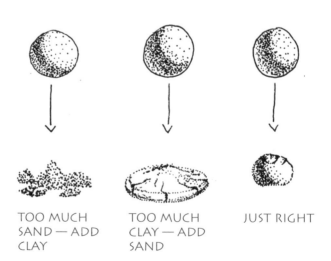

TOO MUCH SAND — ADD CLAY

TOO MUCH CLAY — ADD SAND

JUST RIGHT

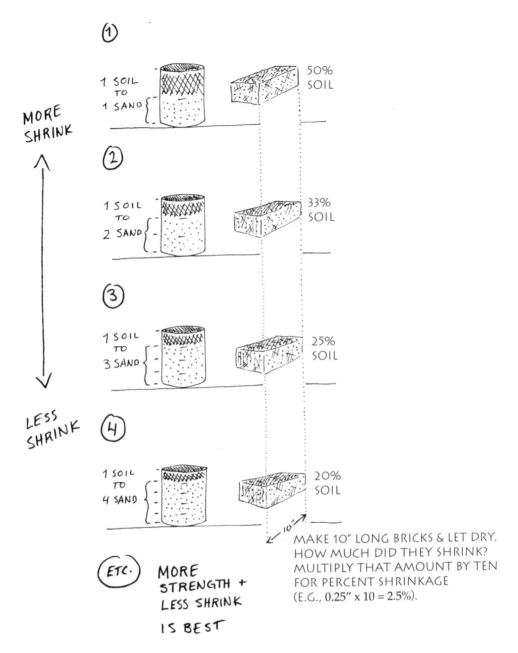

① 1 SOIL TO 1 SAND { — 50% SOIL

MORE SHRINK ↑

② 1 SOIL TO 2 SAND { — 33% SOIL

③ 1 SOIL TO 3 SAND { — 25% SOIL

LESS SHRINK ↓

④ 1 SOIL TO 4 SAND { — 20% SOIL

⟵ 10" ↗

MAKE 10" LONG BRICKS & LET DRY.
HOW MUCH DID THEY SHRINK?
MULTIPLY THAT AMOUNT BY TEN
FOR PERCENT SHRINKAGE
(E.G., 0.25" x 10 = 2.5%).

(ETC.) MORE STRENGTH + LESS SHRINK

IS BEST

TEST YOUR SAMPLE MIXES FOR STRENGTH AND SHRINKAGE

The best way to find a perfect mix is to make loaves, or "bricks," dry them, and see how they hold up. Using your measured, sample mixes, make a series of well-compacted "bricks" — by hand, in a plastic container, a loaf tin, or a wood frame. Don't make them too wet, and don't add straw, as that only makes it harder to see cracks and test for strength. The "bricks" should be at least an inch thick, and at least ten inches long. Clearly mark off ten inches on each brick, and let dry (in a warm oven if you're in a hurry and it's raining). How much did they shrink? If your marks are now only nine inches apart, you had ten percent shrink. Try for two or three percent. Test them for strength with a simple "squeeze test" (next page).

THIS IS A
SQUEEZE
TEST, N<u>O</u>T A
B E N D I N G
TEST

STRENGTH TESTING

Squeeze a corner of a brick between your fingers. Does it crumble, or is it hard as rock? The trick here is to apply compressive force *without* bending. (Even the strongest concrete won't take much bending — that's why we have re-bar, and it's also why buildings of earth usually have straw mixed in.)

The best mix is the strongest, with the least shrinkage and cracking.

Builders using earth for structural components of inhabited earthen buildings use the same basic tests, but employ more precise machines and methods to measure the strength of their building mix against much more rigorous and scientific criteria.

You should be able to get a good enough feel by hand, but you can also try stepping on a sample, or hitting it with something hard.

A COLLABORATIVE
OVEN ON AN
"URBANITE"
FOUNDATION
A member of the community where this was built was kind enough to let me know about it. It was a joint project of students of Culture, Ecology and Sustainable Community at New College in Santa Rosa, California, and a non-profit youth services program called "Kid's Street." The site is a community garden. (Photo courtesy B. Sundstrom)

STEP TWO: FOUNDATION & FLOOR

Your foundation needs to do four things:

1. support the weight of the oven;
2. keep the whole structure rigid, so it won't shift when the ground gets wet or freezes;
3. protect against ground moisture and rain;
4. raise the oven to a good working height (a low foundation is easier to build and perfectly adequate for occasional baking, but if you use it a lot, you'll want the oven floor about waist high).

For now, I'll describe a foundation of "urbanite," or concrete chunks, but the same basic procedure applies to rock, block, brick, railroad ties, etc. (For more foundation ideas, see Chapter Five.)

DIGGING YOUR FOUNDATION HOLE

Mark out a four and a half foot circle where your oven will be. Unless you're building directly on an existing concrete pad or driveway, dig down to the frost line (ask a local contractor how deep that is). The bottom of the hole should be firm and solid; if necessary, tamp it down with a 2x4, pole, or other implement that you can use piston-fashion for ramming.

Fill the hole to ground level with drain rock and rubble (or anything that will be firm, but allow water to drain — if you have masses of urbanite, use that; fill gaps with sand or gravel rather than soil, if you can. Otherwise, don't worry.) Round drain rock or dry sand will settle quite well by itself, but if it feels soft, tamp it solid.

If you're building on very wet ground, you may want to dig a drain trench (with or without plastic drain pipe at the bottom), to lead water down and away from your oven site. "Drain to daylight" if you can (in other words, to a place where water will flow away naturally). If you're building on a slope, make sure you level off the material in your foundation hole. Use a spirit level if you like, but for such a small foundation, trust your eyes — their accuracy may surprise you.

Lay out a first course in a four foot ring, at least a foot wide. Fill the ring with rubble, sand, or gravel. Lay the second course on top of the first, being sure to stagger your joints like bricks, "one over two," as old-timer wall-builders said. If it seems wobbly, make a mortar of about one part mud to three or four parts sand (the same mix you'll use for the first layer of the oven), or use commercial cement mortar if you prefer. If you're short on rock, you can make a cob foundation on top of a single course of rock; just make sure there's no way for dampness to creep up into the cob.

Filling your foundation with drain rock ensures that water won't migrate up into the oven base. It is important to have this "capillary break" between an earthen structure and the ground — at least six inches worth. (If you're short on rock, rubble, or sand, the rest of the foundation *can* be filled with soil, but it should be tamped down *very well*, otherwise it will settle, and your oven will sink.) Fill the foundation not quite to the top. The last four inches or so will be filled with sand for your subfloor.

A FOUNDATION ON LEVEL GROUND (IN A NO-FROST ZONE)

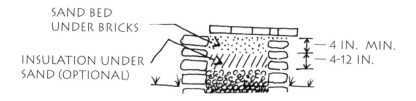

SAND BED
UNDER BRICKS

INSULATION UNDER
SAND (OPTIONAL)

— 4 IN. MIN.
— 4-12 IN.

A FOUNDATION ON SLOPING GROUND IN A FROST ZONE

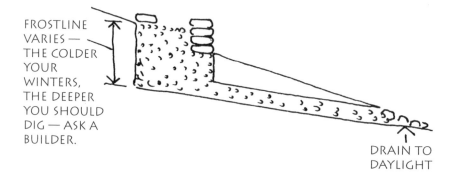

FROSTLINE VARIES — THE COLDER YOUR WINTERS, THE DEEPER YOU SHOULD DIG — ASK A BUILDER.

DRAIN TO DAYLIGHT

LAY YOUR SUBFLOOR

The floor of your oven needs to be thick and dense to store plenty of heat for baking. The simplest and easiest thing to do is simply to set your floor bricks (or tile) in a four to six inch bed of sand. The thickness of the sand isn't critical, since you'll have plenty of dense rock and rubble under your floor as well, but it should be at least an inch or two so that you can make a nice, smooth, flat bed in which to set your bricks.

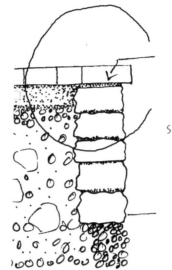

The sand bed should come up level to, or just above the top of the foundation ring, so your floor bricks can extend out into the hearth area in front of the door, without running into an uneven surface. Now you're ready to set your floor.

EXTEND YOUR SAND BED OVER THE FOUNDATION IF YOU'LL BE SETTING BRICKS THERE

LAY BRICKS FOR YOUR OVEN FLOOR

Your floor will be subject to huge stresses: tremendous heat, scraping and gouging from metal tools, banging and poking from bits of firewood — so set the bricks carefully! Also, the more even and flat your floor, the easier the cleaning — and the cleaner your floor, the less chance of finding ash or grit in your bread.

Set your bricks in fine sand so they settle level and solid. If your sand is coarse (grains 1/8 of an inch or larger), screen out the coarsest stuff with an old window screen. Give yourself a half inch of fine sand. Using a straight-edged board, gently scrape the surface flat and smooth. Flat, smooth, and even is more important than dead level. If you're not sure how the bricks should be placed to make the shape you want, lay them out on the ground first. Then locate the center of the foundation and lay those bricks first — if you don't, an off-center floor would give you uneven walls, and uneven baking.

LOCATE THE CENTER (X) OF YOUR FOUNDATION AND START LAYING BRICKS FROM THERE

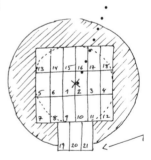

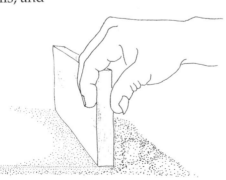

NOTE: IF YOUR FOUNDATION IS VERY BIG, YOU MAY NEED TO EXTEND THE TONGUE IN ORDER FOR IT TO OVERHANG.

The bricks will be surrounded and held in place by the heavy, solid ring of the oven walls. No mortar is necessary. In fact, mortar would make a tough job of replacing worn or broken bricks in the future. And no matter how well built, your oven's floor will eventually crack and deteriorate (depending on how much you use it). So if you were to set the bricks in mortar, they'd be very hard, if not impossible, to remove.

Make sure the bricks are set tight against each other, with no cracks or gaps. Holding the next brick level and about an inch above the sand, gently "kiss" its long side to the matching side of the previous one. Slide it down 'til it's flat and firm on the sand. Once it's set, don't wiggle it! You'll only open the gap and let sand in.

When all the bricks are down, including the hearth "tongue," set them firmly in their beds by tapping each brick face lightly with the handle end of a hammer. Make sure all are well seated and flush with their neighbors. If a brick stands up a bit proud of its neighbors, tap it down. If they all don't sit firm, flat, and tight, take 'em apart, re-smooth the sand, and try again. The second time goes easier.

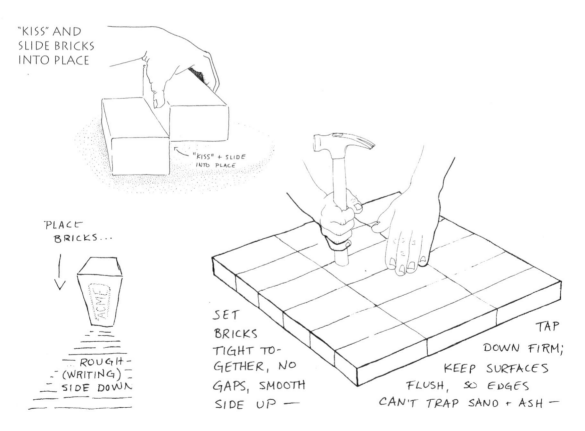

"KISS" AND SLIDE BRICKS INTO PLACE

"KISS" + SLIDE INTO PLACE

PLACE BRICKS...

ROUGH- (WRITING) SIDE DOWN

SET BRICKS TIGHT TO-GETHER, NO GAPS, SMOOTH SIDE UP —

TAP DOWN FIRM; KEEP SURFACES FLUSH, SO EDGES CAN'T TRAP SAND + ASH —

STEP THREE: MAKE A SAND FORM, OR SHAPE THE VOID

The oven is just a void, and the sand form is what will give it shape. Once built, you'll cut a door in the hard shell of the oven and dig out the sand. Draw a circle all the way to the very edges of your floor, to make the best use of every brick (a string tied to a pencil makes a good compass — put the other end of the string at the center, and hold it under your thumb while you swing an arc). Make a dome of sand out to the mark; only corner bricks should show. The sand should be moist enough to pack into a ball, but not so wet that it slumps. If it's too coarse and won't hold its shape even when damp, you can add a little clay (but make sure your sand isn't too wet, because clay will only make it wetter). Make a test dome with the clay mix and adjust 'til it's right.

SHAPING THE VOID*

* " IT'S THE VOID IN THE VESSEL THAT MAKES IT VALUABLE "

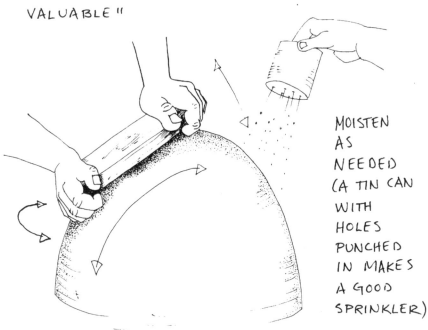

MOISTEN AS NEEDED (A TIN CAN WITH HOLES PUNCHED IN MAKES A GOOD SPRINKLER)

"WALK" A BOARD ALL AROUND THE FORM TO MAKE IT FIRM, SMOOTH, + BEAUTIFUL

You can go up in layers or build out from a central pile. You want the walls near vertical at first, so the tops of your loaves don't hit the wall as they rise. (Imagine your hemispherical dome sitting on "walls" four inches high.) All in all, it should be a bit higher than the radius of the oven floor. Remember, the radius is half the diameter of a circle. A 27 inch diameter oven, with a 13-1/2 inch radius, should be 16-20 inches high. Much higher, and you get cooling eddies at the top of the dome; lower, and the fire can't get enough air. The dome should be even, hard packed, and solid. Make it beautiful. Imagine flames roiling around in your void.

MEASURE THE HEIGHT OF YOUR OVEN, & MAKE A PARTING LAYER

When you're satisfied with your sand dome, take a straight stick and hold it level across the top of your dome. Measure the distance between the stick and the oven floor. This will be the interior height of your oven dome. Multiply it by 63% (0.63) to determine the proper height for your oven door (you'll cut it out in Step Six). Write down the number!

In a dark oven, it can sometimes be hard to know if you're digging out the sand form, or digging into the oven wall. So ease removal of the sand form by covering the dome with a layer or two of wet newspaper. Make thin strips if big sheets are too hard to work with. Smooth them down flat. Or use thin plastic. Or dead leaves. Any stray bits you can't remove will burn out.

(B. Steen photo.)

DOME HEIGHT IS 60-75% OF DOME DIAMETER.

←— DIAMETER —→

DOOR HEIGHT IS 63% OF DOME HEIGHT.

100%   63%

DOOR HEIGHT IS 63% OF DOME HEIGHT.

WHY 63%?

Researchers examined hundreds of Canadian clay ovens and found that the average door height in the best ovens was consistently 63% of the height of the interior dome. Inferior ovens compensated for badly formed domes with rear vents to aid draft & combustion. See The Bread Ovens of Quebec, *by Boily and Blanchette.*

STEP FOUR: MIX MUD!

MAKING "COB" FOR THE FIRST, OR THERMAL LAYER

You're ready to mix your first batch of cob. The only difference between this and what you'd use to build a house is the absence of straw. No straw means a denser mix that will store as much heat as possible. Use the proportions you've figured out from your testing.

Prepare a pile of dry mix on your tarp. Use five-gallon buckets to measure. Start with a three or four bucket mix. You probably won't want to mix more than a full wheelbarrow load, or about five buckets.

Mixing is easy with two people, each holding two corners of the tarp. With feet spread, knees bent, elbows down and shoulders back, roll the mix from side to side. Don't try to lift it off the ground, but just roll one half onto the other until it looks homogenous. (You can also do this solo by pulling one end of the tarp over the other, rolling the mix as you go. In this case a longer tarp is much easier. Or just use bare hands and feet and muck around in it.)

MIXING MUD
WITH A TARP:
*Lean back, keep your
spine straight — let
your legs do the work.*
(B. Steen photo.)

BUILD YOUR OWN EARTH OVEN

Make a big hole in the middle of your pile, fill it less than half full with water, and push the dry mix slowly into the water until it disappears. Spare the water. It's easy to add, but hard to take away.

Mix again with the tarp. Resist the temptation to add water. When it starts to clump, like dough for pie crust, take off your shoes, jump in, and do the twist — seriously! As you twist and turn, your feet work like rotating pistons, breaking up the clay and pressing sand into it. But don't *be* serious! Play music! Grab a partner! Dance until each grain is well coated with a layer of sticky clay. With enough packing (50-100 pats from hand to hand) it should pack into a hard ball. If it won't, add just a little water, and mix again. Not to worry if it's too wet; you can either add dry mix (harder), or use as is and allow more drying time (easier).

DO THE TWIST!

(*H. Field photo.*)

STEP FIVE: APPLY LAYERS

When your mix is ready, start pressing handfuls around the base of your sand form. Press the mix down with thumbs and fingers so you don't damage your sand form. If you press into the form it will crack and break, so press the mix into itself, almost as if the form wasn't there. This will maintain the form's integrity, and ensure that each handful of mix is well integrated with the rest. Make a layer at least three inches thick. Measure your fingers to see how many inches across they are. Use them to guide you in maintaining thickness. If you want the oven to stay hot longer, you can make it thicker, but remember that a thicker oven will require more fuel.

Use small amounts of material, and take care not to leave voids or soft spots where the mix meets the sand form. Don't slap or pat the mix, it only weakens it. Use your hands to maintain a well-defined edge. As you go higher, the face of the layer should angle upwards (see diagram next page). Keep making mixes until you've covered the whole form, even where the door will go (you'll cut it out later).

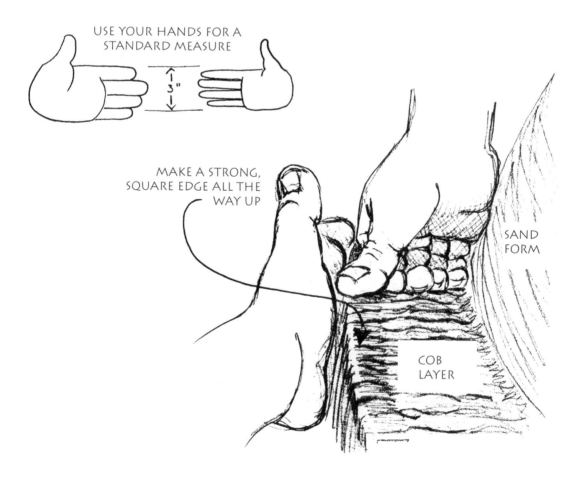

USE YOUR HANDS FOR A STANDARD MEASURE

3"

MAKE A STRONG, SQUARE EDGE ALL THE WAY UP

SAND FORM

COB LAYER

When the form is covered, take a flat board, scrap of 2x4, or what-have-you, and pack the material, whacking it firmly with the board. It should go hard and smooth, and sound solid. If it squishes out from under and/or it sticks to the board, your mix was a bit too damp — but don't worry! Instead of whacking, rock the board firmly back and forth, up and down, the same way you did on your sand form. Or try rubbing it in small circles to consolidate and compact everything. When it's beautiful and firm, roughen the surface — scratch it all around with a fork or a sharp stick, to help the next layer stick.

Say your dome is 18 inches high. The height of your door should be 0.63 x 18, or 11.25 inches. You don't want your door too wide or you'll lose heat; too narrow, and you won't be able to maneuver things in and out. I have had good luck with a door width of three firebricks (3 x 4.5, or13.5 inches).

Mark the top center of the door, and scratch a rough outline into the mud mix. If your mix was good and dry and you successfully compacted it, you can cut your door and pull out the sand form immediately! Start by cutting a hole just big enough to get your hand in. Dig a narrow channel to see if the thermal layer is stiff enough to hold. When you poke it with a finger, it should be firm and resist denting. When in doubt, wait! You can speed up drying by digging your narrow channel further into the sand form, to allow more air circulation. Don't dig out too much though, because wet mixes do fall, especially with a flat dome or in a big oven. But if it does, don't worry. The second time is easier! (Read Step Six for more on carving the door.)

MAINTAIN THE INTEGRITY OF YOUR SAND FORM

NO

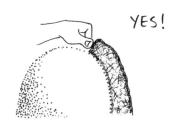

YES!

PRESS MUD AGAINST ITSELF, NOT AGAINST THE SAND FORM

ONE

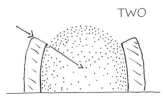

TWO

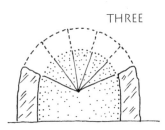

THREE

MORE LAYERS

The thick earthen walls of traditional earthen ovens hold lots of heat, and can bake for hours on a single firing. The second layer adds mass to your oven and gives you something to sculpt, if you want to make a sculpted oven. This layer can be three to six inches thick, and is made of the same stuff as the first layer, but wetter, and with lots of straw. (Or, if you want to insulate, you would use a lighter material instead of cob; read Chapter Five.)

Make the mud mix as before, but wetter (not so wet that it won't hold its shape — a bit drier than peanut butter: stiff, but still smooshy). Tread it out into a big pancake, and sprinkle a thin layer of straw all over. Tread and turn (pull it over with the tarp), 'til it's well integrated. Add more straw and do it again. It should start to roll up into a big burrito. When you can stand on the roll and only sink a couple of inches, it's ready.

Cover the rest of the oven: Except for compacting it with a stick, cover the oven with this mix the same way you did the first layer. Use your flat stick to refine the form, rocking it around the way you did the sand form (but not compacting). Make sure your cob shell is an even thickness. Leave a rough surface to give the final plaster a good "key" to hold onto.

STEP SIX: CUT DOOR & REMOVE SAND

This step can actually come before you add more layers, or after. It depends largely on how wet or dry you material is. When you think it's time to remove the sand form, first carve out the door just shy of your line, working from the center. Use a metal bladed tool — a dull knife, big metal spoon, mason's trowel, or what-have-you. Leave the opening a bit small; you'll refine it later.

Remove the sand. Use your hands as much as possible, since you may not notice when a stick or other tool starts chipping away at the inside layer of your oven. As you dig out the bottom, sand will fall on its own. Long arms and a flashlight may help for the far reaches. Peel away the newspaper and refine the doorway so it's smooth and even (try polishing the edges with the back of a spoon to make them smooth and hard). You're ready for your next step!

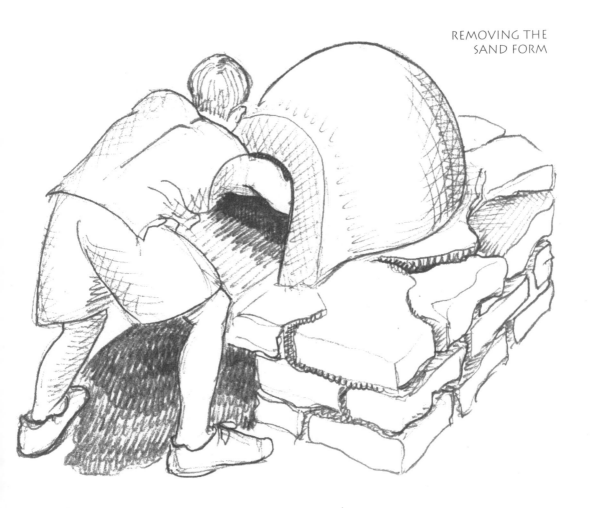

REMOVING THE
SAND FORM

STEP SEVEN:
FINISH PLASTERS & SCULPTING

Your first (and necessary) sculpture is the basic oven form itself. But even if you go no further, it's worth finishing it 'til it's beautiful, so it can give you pleasure every time you look at it. If you're inspired to make a more involved sculpture, see "variations" for tips and ideas. But read here first about basic techniques, which you'll use in any case.

You may have already smoothed the surface of your second layer with a board or metal trowel — wetting and "polishing" the mud. If so, you may be done. If not, or if you want to make more detailed sculptural decorations, you'll want to mix a fine plaster that holds detail better.

SCULPTING
BASIC LINES
AND PLANE
CHANGES
A spoon makes a great tool, and they come in all different sizes! (B. Steen photo)

BUILD YOUR OWN EARTH OVEN

MIXING PLASTERS

Plaster requires shorter straw and more water for a more spreadable mixture than cob. Otherwise, it should be the same proportion of sand to clay as you used in your first (and perhaps second) layers. Again, if your sand is coarse, you may want to screen out the big bits, or use finer sand (a sharp-edged mason's sand is best for strength, but beach sand will make decent plaster in a pinch).

A barn floor covered with loose straw is an easy source of short bits. Or chop handfuls of long straw into two to three inch lengths with a machete or hatchet on a chopping block — watch your fingers! If you have a weed whacker, make an oversize blender with a garbage can about 1/3 full of straw ("pulsing" it on and off). To make a superfine mix, rub handfuls of chopped straw against a 1/4 or 1/2 inch screen to filter out the long bits.

A FINE COLLECTION OF EXPENSIVE, HARD-TO-FIND SCULPTING TOOLS ...

The very finest plasters are made with fresh horse or cow manure (cow is finer). Those animals not only chop the fiber, but digest the softer material, and deposit the more fibrous stuff in a nice, moist form that is naturally adhesive. Manure is treasured by many peoples, not only for fuel and fertilizer, but also for finishing buildings. Some make floors of pure, fresh manure — spread, smoothed like concrete, and left to dry. If you've ever kicked an old dry cow pie, you'll appreciate its potential. (Note that the bagged manure sold in garden centers is aged and composted, so the fibers are all broken down — no good for plaster.)

Fresh manure smells strong but not unpleasant. Use rubber gloves if you're worried about potential pathogens (most U.S. livestock get better health care than the majority of humans, but manure *can* carry e. coli and salmonella, so wash well and be careful about where you put dirty hands, gloves, boots, etc.). For a less pungent and more benign mix, use dry manure; soak it in water or grate it on a piece of 1/8" screen. Other short fibers that might work include cattail fuzz, pet hair, dryer lint, and what-have-you. You can also make colored plasters with naturally colored clays.

WORKING PLASTER

This is pure pleasure, like icing a cake or finger-painting. Schmear it onto the oven in handfuls. Work from the bottom up. Sometimes it goes easier if you schmear it just once, not again and again. If it still seems too soft and flexible after it's dried, add another layer.

Final finishing can be done wet or dry, depending on what you want. A brush dragged over a wet surface makes a lovely texture that will vary with the stiffness of the bristles and the wetness of the mud. Try a whisk broom. See what the light does when you drag it one way and then the other. Make patterns.

If you want a harder, "polished" finish, wait 'til the mud is stiff, like leather, but still dark with moisture (if you're not sure, test it out). Find a hand-sized scrap of smooth wood and rub it on the plaster in small circles. Wet the trowel or the surface of the plaster (a spray bottle works great). The smoother your tool, the finer the finish. A metal trowel will give you a much different texture than wood.

Experiment. Scratch designs into the surface with a fork. Press the bowl of a spoon into it and see what it looks like. Try the end of a board. Anything you can bring to hand can be a tool.

DRYING

Air drying the oven can take weeks, but if you're impatient to bake, make a small fire in the oven to speed up the process. Ovens can be quick-dried without damage, but they may crack. If so, don't worry. Cracking due to natural expansion invariably occurs during firing. If the cracks don't close when the oven is cool, you can fill them (from the outside) with cob or clay.

DETAIL: DOOR
OPENING & BAKING DOOR
Easier to fit the door at this stage, and then build on accordingly. The nails provide a "key" to help bond the next layer of cob.

STEP 8: MAKE A DOOR FOR BAKING

The basic, chimney-less oven is fired without a door. Only when you've cleaned out the fire and loaded your loaves do you need to seal the oven shut.

A wood door is probably easiest to make (though I've shut up a hot oven with bricks and sand, or whatever else I could get my hands on). It doesn't even need to fit perfectly, since you'll drape it with a wet cloth to keep it from charring and to add steam for baking. You can also soak it in water, or screw a sheet of aluminum to the inside surface of the door, or wrap it in foil to reflect heat back into the oven.

If you want to make a tight-fitting door, make an accurate template of the opening with a scissors and piece of paper or cardboard. Trace the template onto a piece (or pieces) of wood, and cut to shape. Try to cut the edge of the wood and door frame at matching angles, like the top of a Halloween pumpkin, so the door won't fall into the oven. Better to cut it a bit big than too small — and better to carve away mud than to add it. (If your door does come out a bit small, however, fill the door frame with mud plaster as needed.)

If you're not happy working with wood, you might want to cut a square oven opening so you don't have to worry about making a rounded wooden door. Plywood is not advisable, as the glues would probably give off nasty fumes when heated. A handle can be as simple as a chunk of wood screwed or nailed on. You're ready to fire your oven, and bake!

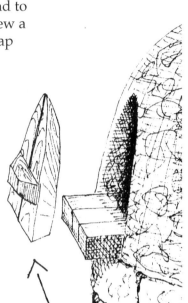

A TWO PIECE
PLANK DOOR JOINED
BY A HANDLE PIECE

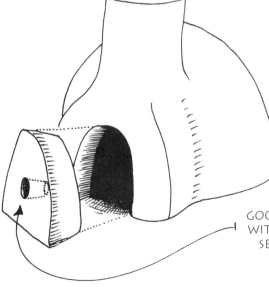

YOU CAN ALSO MAKE A DOOR OUT OF COB (ESPECIALLY GOOD FOR AN OVEN WITH A CHIMNEY — SEE CHAPTER FIVE).

THE BREAD IS READY TO BAKE NOW!

Pulling the remains of a fire with a shovel. The monkey oven was built in the center of a cob bake house as part of an exhibit called "Earthworks: a celebration of the terrestrial imagination." We taught a workshop for about fifteen people. In five days we built the oven, and the five-foot high walls of a sixteen foot diameter bake house — all by hand and foot! The oven and most of the other sculpting on the building was done by participating kids. (D. Lesley photo.)

CHAPTER TWO: FIRING & BAKING IN YOUR OVEN

You will learn best how your oven works by using it. Intuitive, experiential knowledge is most effective, if not (and perhaps because it's not) always precise. Try the following to get started:

1. **USE SCRAP OR "WASTE" WOOD.** You want a quick hot fire more than a long, slow burn. In the old days, a few "faggots," or small bundles of brush would fire an oven, and they were easily gathered off the floor of the forest or in hedgerows. Softwood or hardwood is fine, although hardwood will give more heat. Pruning from trees or yard shrubs work great (provided, of course, they're dry). Look around your yard, or follow landscape or city maintenance crews and ask if you can haul stuff away before they run it through their chipper. Lumber scraps are fine, provided they're not pressure-treated or painted with poisonous stuff. You can also burn natural gas or propane. Talk to your supplier.

2. **DRY YOUR FUEL.** Wet wood won't really start to provide heat until it's dry, and it takes lots of energy to dry it. Better to stack your wood, cover it, and let sun, wind, and time dry it thoroughly (for free!) If you do have to burn wet wood, allow for more fuel, more smoke, and more time to reach baking temperature.

3. **USE THIN PIECES** (wrist thick); the increased surface area of the wood makes for a faster, hotter burn. It's also generally more effective to burn one or two large loads of wood than many small ones.

4. **FIRE "BREATHES" — GIVE IT AIR.** Stack the wood loosely. Build in an air channel, front to back. This can be right down the center, or to one side. Lots of smoke means it's choking. Move the wood. Small adjustments make a big difference. Play with it. In general, you should start your fire in front, push it back, adding longer pieces later; let the fire burn all the way to the back of the oven before adding more fuel. When it's almost to temperature, you can spread out the coals thicker at the sides and thinner in the middle (where the oven is already hot). Letting the coals burn down can add significant heat to the oven. It will also lengthen your firing time in case your bread needs more time to rise.

While an efficient fire burns with the least smoke, an earthen oven is not the most efficient furnace — smoke is part of the process — that's why you built the door away from the wind. If gusty wind makes smoke a real problem, set bricks up around the oven mouth to deflect gusts and improve draft; you might want to consider adding a chimney (see Chapter Five).

5. **LEARN HOW TIME AND TEMPERATURE RELATE.** You need 450 degrees to bake bread. An oven two to three feet in diameter heats up to baking temps in one to three hours. Various gauges can help you measure temperature.

    Feel the outside surface with your hand. Watch the inside surface. When the temperature reaches about 700° Fahrenheit, the black soot will burn off and the interior surface will be a deep, glowing red. Depending on the thickness of you oven and the length of your fire, this will help you decide when it's time to pull the fire. A hi-tech pyrometer is more precise, but very expensive.

6. **REMOVE THE REMAINS OF THE FIRE.** At this point, it's reached temperature and you hope to have only coals left. Or maybe you still have burning sticks. Either way, use a hoe, shovel, or proper "rooker" (see below for more on oven tools) to scrape coals and ash into a metal bucket, a Weber-type grill, or other nonflammable container (not a plastic bucket or garbage can!). Be careful around the inside corners of the oven where it's easy to cause damage. Also beware burning your hands or feet on hot oven walls or little hot coals that fall on the ground. You may want to wear oven mitts or heavy leather gloves.

    Clean the oven floor with something damp (not dripping wet) and not synthetic — no plastic brushes, no polyester rags! Cotton, burlap, hemp, sisal, or other natural bristle only. If you haven't made a proper scuffle, use an old cotton rag or mop or natural fiber scrub brush nailed to a stick.

7. **"SOAK" YOUR OVEN.** Not with water, but with heat. At this point, your floor and ceiling will be at different temperatures. If you let them sit for a while, all the inside temperatures will even out. It's best, now, to close the door opening with a piece of sheet metal, cookie-tray, or other non-flammable barrier, to prevent unnecessary airflow and cooling. (See Chapter Five on chimneys and doors.) Soaking times will vary from oven to oven. Start with 15 minutes to 1/2 hour. If it still seems too hot, of if your bread still needs to rise, soak it longer.

8. **TEST FOR TEMPERATURE.** With practice, you'll learn to recognize baking temps by feel. You can use a standard oven thermometer, but I like more direct methods. Toss a handful of flour onto the oven floor. At bread temperature, it will brown quickly (10-20 seconds), and then blacken. It if chars or smokes instantly, your oven is too hot, or needs more soak time, or both.

   Hand testing: carefully put your closed fist into the oven door and count off as long as you can stand. I find that an eight-count works for me ("one-one-hundred, two-one-hundred..."). You can practice, and get a sense of how 600 or 400 degrees feels, by doing the same thing in a gas or electric oven.

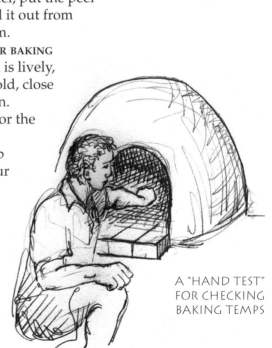

RAKING COALS OUT
OF A HOT OVEN

9. **LOAD YOUR LOAVES.** Traditionally, bakers use a "peel" to place loaves directly on the oven floor, but you can use just about any narrow board or even a piece of stiff cardboard. Sprinkle it with a little coarse corn meal (Malt-O-Meal works too), to help the loaves slide. If you rise your loaves in baskets, turn them out directly onto the peel. If you rise them on a board, pick them up gently, perhaps using a dough knife underneath. Place loaf on peel; put the peel where you want the loaf, and briskly pull it out from under. Quickly seal the door to trap steam.

10. **ADJUST TIME AND TEMPERATURE TO SUIT YOUR BAKING NEEDS.** If it's a warm day and your dough is lively, start your fire early. If it's sluggish and cold, close up your oven and let the coals burn down. Better to have the oven hot and waiting for the bread than have the dough going slack because the oven needs to cool. Also keep in mind that you can do a lot more in your oven than bake bread. You can plan your menu of the day or the week to match the heat-retention properties of your oven. Cookies and pies don't cook as hot as bread. Bread doesn't cook as hot as pizza. So start with pizza for dinner at 650° F., then bread, potatoes, beans, vegetables, pies and cookies, crackers,

A "HAND TEST"
FOR CHECKING
BAKING TEMPS

granola, rice pudding; roast nuts and beans (bean flour makes a great, quick-cooking soup base, as well as bean-cakes and falafel), and finally, dry fruit or make yogurt. You can also use the last heat of the oven to dry the wood for the next firing (if you don't use the higher heat for baking, however, and the oven is quite hot, drying wood can produce volatile gases. Be careful; when in doubt leave the door open).

A NOTE ON PIZZA: At 700 degrees (about as hot as your oven will get) pizza will cook in two to three minutes. (So will pita bread.) It's easy to cook one or two pizzas as soon as you've pulled the fire out of the oven. However, if you want to make more, you'll need a small fire at the side of the oven to make a bright flame to maintain that 700 degree heat for cooking the tops of the pizzas. Since it's easy to bring a warm oven back up to temperature with a small fire, Dan Wing suggests baking bread before you have your pizza party, re-lighting the fire, and then making pizza.

Buon appetito!

TIPPING A WELL-PROOFED LOAF OUT OF ITS RISING BASKET ONTO A PEEL, SLASHING THE DOUGH WITH A SHARP KNIFE, AND LOADING THE LOAF INTO THE OVEN TO BAKE.

BUILD YOUR OWN EARTH OVEN

ASSEMBLING A SET OF TRADITIONAL BAKING TOOLS

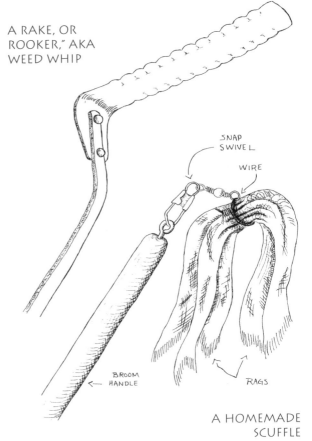

A RAKE, OR ROOKER," AKA WEED WHIP

SNAP SWIVEL

WIRE

BROOM HANDLE →

RAGS

A HOMEMADE SCUFFLE

- **A RAKE OR ROOKER** is an "L" shaped piece of metal that you use to pull out whatever coals and embers remain in the oven at the end of firing. An old weed whip is perfect for the job. An old hoe can also stand in for a rooker.
- **A SCUFFLE** is an elegantly simple tool that you can make by twisting a stout screw-eye into the end of an old broomstick. Attach a heavy-duty snap swivel (size 1/0 from the fishing tackle store), and to the end of that, use a length of wire to attach clean toweling or rags. The swivel allows the rags to spin freely. Wet and wring them out, and with a gentle circular motion, "scuffle" around the floor of the oven, whisking it clean of ash and grit, even deep in the corners.
- **A PEEL** is like a canoe paddle, but with a thinner blade (1/2 inch at the handle to 1/4 inch or less at the tip). Some peels (such as are used for unloading hot pizza) are metal, to resist burning. Wood or metal, you can buy them ready made in different sizes from fancy catalog suppliers, kitchen stores, and the like. Or make one to your own specifications at home. For most home-sized loaves, a six-inch-wide peel is plenty. If you make a wide pizza peel, make sure it's narrow enough to fit in your oven door. If you're short on tools and woodworking experience, nail a piece of thin masonite or plywood to a handle, and call it good (you'll still want to make a sharp edge to slide easily under a cooked loaf). If you

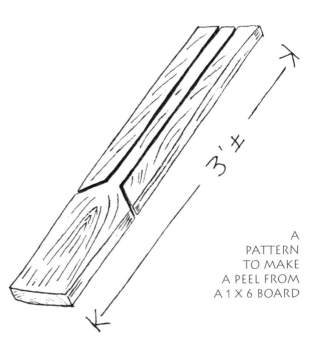

3' ±

A PATTERN TO MAKE A PEEL FROM A 1 X 6 BOARD

want a more elegant tool, find a straight-grained, 1x6 inch, hard or softwood board (soft pine or fir will be easier to work). The length should equal the depth of your oven, plus a foot or two or more depending on how big and hot your oven is — but make it longer at first, and cut it down as needed. Trace and cut out the shape. You don't need a fancy saw if a handsaw is all you have: cut the blade square, almost down to the handle. Then cut (or if the wood is straight-grained enough, split) out the handle. Round off square edges with a knife, hatchet, drawknife, plane, saw, or rasp. In the same way, thin the bottom of the blade until it seems sharp enough.

USE A KNIFE, PLANE, CHISEL, OR SAW TO GIVE YOUR PEEL A SHARP, SHOVEL-LIKE EDGE

- **RISING BASKETS** can be had at great expense from fancy suppliers. Made of willow and linen, imported from Europe, and priced at about $30 each, they perform perfectly and are very lovely. But plain wicker baskets seven to eight inches across work just as well. They might cost a buck at craft, import, or thrift stores. You can also use plastic or metal bowls lined with cotton or linen cloth.

Insulated, heat-resistant gloves are good for making pizza, or when you have to reach deep into a hot oven. Leather welding gloves or fireproof kiln-gloves work — try a welding or ceramic supply house.

- **A BRASS BRISTLE BRUSH** is necessary for cleaning burnt cheese and corn meal off the oven floor when cooking pizza, but some people like to use them prior to scuffling. Buy one from a restaurant supplier.

- **A PORTABLE KNEADING TABLE** with three high sides contains flying flour when kneading or shaping loaves. Nice for small kitchens without much counter space. Find a solid board the right size for your space (plywood works well, and a hard veneer on top is nice). Frame it on three sides with a six-inch-high rail about an inch thick.

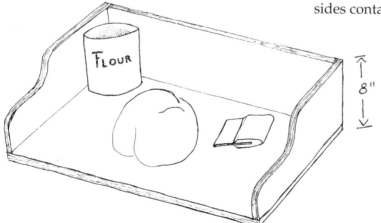

FLOUR

8"

BAKING TIME IS
AN EVENT...

...ESPECIALLY
WHEN THE LOAVES
COME OUT.

CHAPTER TWO: FIRING AND BAKING IN YOUR OVEN   49

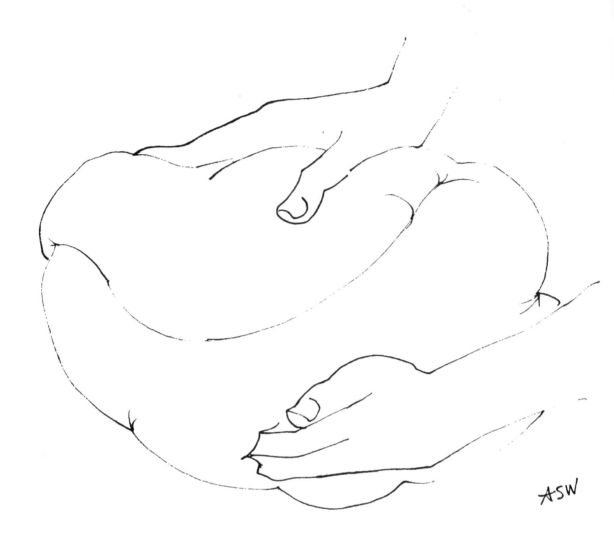

WORK IS LOVE MADE VISIBLE. AND IF YOU CANNOT
WORK WITH LOVE, BUT ONLY WITH DISTASTE, IT IS
BETTER THAT YOU SHOULD LEAVE YOUR WORK AND
SIT AT THE GATE OF THE TEMPLE AND TAKE
ALMS OF THOSE WHO WORK WITH JOY. FOR IF
YOU BAKE BREAD WITH INDIFFERENCE, YOU
BAKE A BITTER BREAD THAT FEEDS BUT HALF
OUR HUNGER.
      — KAHLIL GIBRAN, THE PROPHET

CHAPTER THREE: SIMPLE SOURDOUGH BREAD!

The process of bread making is simple. The science can be as complex as you have time and inclination for. With that in mind, I've divided this section in four:

1. INTRODUCTION AND A NOTE ON INGREDIENTS
2. TEN STEPS TO REAL SOURDOUGH
3. ON YEAST, FLOUR, AND BREAD
4. HOW IT WORKS — THE TEN STEPS IN DETAIL

My only advice is, read what you need to get started, and then begin! If you're a baker, it may all be old news. If you're fairly new to sourdoughs and feeling hesitant, keep reading! Bread — like dancing — takes practice to get to know your partner (the dough) and the rhythm (your baking schedule).

INTRODUCTION AND...

In the middle of rewriting this book (and after marrying a baker) I decided that I couldn't let Hannah make all the bread, so I decided to do something new, and follow a recipe. The one I chose was for a wonderful, whole-grain sourdough called "desem" (say "day-zum"), which I first encountered at my local food cooperative, in the form of Baldwin Hill Bread. I loved the rich, nutty, almost sweet flavor, the chewy texture, and the fact that it seemed to keep forever without going stale or crumbly. Years later, I found a recipe in the Laurel's Kitchen Bread Book for the very same bread from the same bakery — but was daunted by what seemed like long, complex, and seemingly mystical instructions. Since then I've learned that there's no mystery, just good ingredients and a new dance to learn. So I stepped out to a good start, but my first loaves were dense and sour — not the wonderful stuff of memory. My expectations were, of course, based on other flour, other water, and the work of another person's hands. Despite good instructions, I had stronger than average starter and an overheated proofing environment, so my bread rose too much too fast, and then slumped. And I forgot the salt, which made it slump more!

But it was decent bread, and every loaf is an opportunity to learn and therefore good experience. (In the dictionary, "experience" means "to learn by trying" and is literally "what comes out of fear." So bread can be good for your spiritual

SOURDOUGH
HAIKU

by Bob Carlson

Round bricks, chewy,
sour:
With Tillamook extra-
sharp,
Beer-making goes
well.

Like a map of Mars
Crust craters, canals,
shadows —
why is it so flat?

Marla from Brooklyn
says "you can't buy
bread like that
here." She should
know.

Soaking up the soup,
sour as love-lost
regret, it
fills the empty space.

Short, stout, round,
wrinkled
Like my favorite aunt,
Myrt —
she made good bread,
too.

practice too.) Thom Leonard, author of *The Bread Book* that I followed for my desem, rightly says that there will be as many ways of making bread as there are bakers.

All bakers work with the same basic principles, however: starches, sugars, and proteins in the grain, combined with yeast and water, make bread. The protein (or gluten), is like muscle. It holds everything else together. When warm it relaxes, when cold it contracts. Water, like blood, is the medium of exchange between body and environment. Yeast (and fire) are spirit. Water and spirit combine with dull, dry flour to become living food. Two principles govern the relationships between them: wet and warm work faster and easier; dry, cold, and salt work slower and harder. Keep those in mind, apply as needed, and you'll make good bread (how those principles work is explained in the following sections).

...A NOTE ON INGREDIENTS

Sourdough bread is just flour, water, and salt. What could be simpler?! (Yeast is not really an ingredient, since it is already there, awaiting cultivation.) Simplicity, however, has suffered in our industrial culture, so depending on where and how you live, it may take a bit of work to do things simply.

Water is complicated by large-scale treatment. Chlorine from the purification process can inhibit yeast development. Evaporate it by boiling, or by letting tap water stand overnight.

Flour is complicated by pesticides and industrial farming. Like chlorine, pesticides also inhibit the development of healthy yeast cultures. Organic flour, grown without pesticides, is worth the few extra cents per pound. Not only will it make your bread better, it will also help keep the culture in agriculture. Whole wheat can be wonderful, but try starting with at least 50% white flour to help your yeast and dough mechanisms work better and make a lighter loaf.

Even white flour, however, is not just flour, but "bread flour," "all purpose flour," "pastry flour," and "self-rising flour." All will make bread, but bread flour is so-called because of its higher protein content. More protein makes for better rising action, but also makes tough, heavy cakes and pastry. Pastry flour makes better cakes and pastries because it has less protein; but it makes crumbly, disappointing bread. All-purpose flour, with moderate protein content, is a middle choice which some prefer for bread. Self-rising flour, which contains chemical rising agents like baking soda and powder, is not recommended.

TEN SIMPLE STEPS (& THREE TRICKS) TO REAL SOURDOUGH

1ST TRICK:
CLEAN WATER AND
CLEAN (ORGANIC)
FLOUR.

2ND TRICK:
VIGOROUS
KNEADING — 15
MINUTES, BY THE
CLOCK!

3RD TRICK:
STEAM IN THE
OVEN.

FRIDAY EVENING:
1. Make a wet "sponge" of flour, 1/4-1/2 cup starter (or 1 teaspoon commercial yeast), and water (one-two cups/loaf).
2. Wait. Let yeasts work and grow slowly (overnight).

SATURDAY MORNING:
3. Save a few tablespoons of sponge to "start" your next batch. Feed it a bit of flour and water and store it in the fridge or other cool spot.
4. Add flour and salt (about a teaspoon per loaf) to the remaining sponge.
5. Knead for 15 minutes
6. Wait two to five hours or so.

NOONISH:
7. Shape your dough into loaves.
8. "Proof" your loves and let them rise about two hours.

ABOUT 2 PM:
9. Bake!
10. Wait 20 minutes before eating — the bread is still cooking!

ABOUT 2:30 PM:
YUM! bread — and still warm enough to melt your butter!

ON YEAST, FLOUR, & BREAD

Making ovens and bread, like any other creative act, is a way to participate in life, to learn more, and worry less. Hands and senses teach as much or more than the intellect. When your hands and belly know good bread, you'll respond accordingly. That kind of faith in yourself is a dimension of life and knowledge sorely neglected by industrial, technological culture — with results much more serious than bad bread. For everyone who comes into contact with it, good bread is a salutary antidote to technology and other post-industrial stresses. Indeed, the word bread, at root, means food — but it is also, at root, related to broth, brew, broil, boil, brood, breed, breathe, brawn, braze, breeze, burn, brand, barm, ferment, fervid, fervor, and effervesce!

Modern bread is a domesticated child of wild yeasts. It was "discovered" thousands of years ago at the dawn of agriculture, when we first learned to gather the wild seeds now known and cultivated as wheat, corn, and rice. In ancient Egypt, people cooked cracked and ground wheat into a mush, much like the hot cereal you might eat on a winter morning. They also made that mush into cakes or crackers, cooked on a hot rock, for traveling.

In what I've read about the history of bread, it seems pretty clear that brewing came before baking (after all, you don't need a fire to make beer). Perhaps (after a party) some householder got a batch of brew mixed up with the morning mush, but didn't realize her "mistake" until she tasted how different (and how much better) they tasted. Or maybe it was a case of poverty, and she had to extend her flour with spent mash from pharaoh's brewery.

The important point, however, is a first principle of both bread and beer: grain, water, and temperature (this is a crucial third element), together create a new, and living material. We have learned since then that there is a fourth, microscopic element: yeasts, which are unicellular fungi that digest carbohydrates and proteins, and excrete carbon dioxide, alcohol, and vinegar. The yeast you buy in the store is related to yeasts that lived in the silts of the Nile River basin when pharaohs ruled.

ARDILLA (SQUIRREL) OVEN,
MEXICO, 1997

An experimental oven and environmental education project with children: the fuel goes in, and the chimney vents behind the tail; the loaves enter between the feet; a grate makes it possible to cook over hot coals. In general, additional openings decrease effectiveness by reducing the amount of radiant mass, and introducing cooling drafts, but we wanted to see if we could make an oven that would allow for continuous firing.

FROG OVEN,
OREGON, 1996

A few weeks after the weekend workshop when we built it, the owners sent a note: "Kiko — Roasted sweet potatoes, zucchini & onions in a cumin/ orange juice glaze, with roast garlic pork loin (for the meat eater) and baked apples, then roasted eggplant, squash and leeks, rosemary polenta, herb roasted salmon and peach pie. This morning, cinnamon rolls…."
One person said that the cooperative labor and shared meals reminded her that it didn't have to be the 70s for people to work together happily.

PHOENIX OVEN AND BENCH, BLACK RANGE LODGE, KINGSTON, NM, 1996
The design began with an old southwestern-style adobe oven, or "horno," which needed repair. Curved stone benches on either side suggested a bird. The young woman shown resting in the wing is a proficient sculptor and was first assistant on the project, which involved scores of people over the course of about two weeks.

HOME
While I was building my cob studio (here still unfinished) I didn't have an oven. Hannah and I finally built this one with a fire box under the oven. The foundation is cob, & enough stone to keep ground water from seeping up. Note the work shelf. (For more on the design, see page 90.)

PHOENIX OVEN, REAR VIEW
The site is an old lodge, recently revived as a B&B and educational center for natural building: thus a Phoenix rebirthing itself from the ashes. The oven is in the bird's belly, and smoke vents out the open beak.

BREAD EUPHORIA
Warren Cohen, center, teaches third grade in Tacoma Washington. He and students Michael Kelly and Avery Welkin, built this oven for a class auction. They tested it at a gala house-warming party. Warren said, "all the guests abandoned the beautifully catered food and began devouring plain, simple bread and butter.... People were in fresh baked bread euphoria — a success!"

YOUNG OVEN-
MAKERS & THEIR
TEACHER
*Debbie Murphy's third-
grade class at the
Waldorf School in
Ashland, Oregon
entirely built their own
turtle oven over the
course of a school year.
Debbie wrote that "we
were so excited to have
our first fire in the oven
just before school
ended." They put their
first loaves in a bit soon
so they came out a bit
dark, but "perfect
inside." Anticipation
and impatience often go
together...*

WHY STARTER? HOW CAN I MAKE IT?

Yeasts are common in air and soil, and immensely varied. Commercial yeast, however, is a monoculture — a single strain cultivated on a massive scale. Some suggest that "wheat intolerance" is really an intolerance to commercial yeast. "Wild" sourdoughs may offer relief.

Yeasts will cultivate any fresh dough, given time. All you have to do to make starter is mix flour and water, wait, and watch. It usually takes a week or two to develop a strong starter, and it may not get really good 'til you've baked with it for a while. Starter is generally kept wet and warm (65-85 degrees), but if you're not baking regularly, you can keep dry, cold starter viable a long time (months) as a ball of stiff dough in your fridge. Lower temperatures (50-60 degrees) will also favor different varieties of yeast and produce different flavors. Desem (see below) is a cool temperature yeast culture that makes a "sweeter" bread. Experiment! If you use commercial yeast, and keep it like a starter, you may end up with a wild starter anyway, since studies suggest that, over time, wild yeasts tend to outcompete cultivated yeasts. (*The Bread Builders* has a good discussion of recent yeast research.)

In general, commercial yeast recipes call for significant amounts of oil, sugar, and other amendments. While small amounts of oil can improve bread texture and keeping qualities, larger quantities inhibit yeast. So recipes add more yeast and sugar to overcome inhibitions and make faster bread. In my experience, the result is a cakey kind of bread that is nice at first but weak in the long run, and quick to go crumbly.

On the other hand, naturally leavened breads made with wild yeasts keep extremely well. Store them in a cool, dry place (not the fridge) with the cut edge down, to limit exposure to drying air. Some claim that good whole-wheat sourdough only reaches its best flavor three days after baking. Even after more than a week, a little toasting restores freshness. When it does dry out (I've rarely seen it mold), it makes great bread crumbs, breakfast cereal, fondue, and hardtack (yummy at the bottom of a bowl of hot soup).

FLOUR, CHEMICALS & INDUSTRIAL CULTURE

Commercial flour is typically made with chemically fertilized and treated wheat. Those chemicals can inhibit or prevent the healthy growth of yeasts.

Yeasts are among the simplest of living organisms. Farmers apply pesticides to their crops in order to kill organisms far more complex than yeasts, so it should be no surprise that pesticides discourage healthy yeast cultures. (We ignore the obvious at our own risk.) Even plain table salt can retard (or kill) yeast, which is why you don't add it 'til after the sponge has worked and grown, and you've removed a fresh portion for your next batch.

In addition, organic flours are also somewhat less likely to be made from genetically engineered wheats (at least they should be, if we can maintain decent standards for what is allowed to be sold as "organic"). Although many argue that genetic engineering is little different from the age-old practice of selective breeding, neither selection (nor the more recent phenomenon of hybridization) ever allowed us to combine the genes of a plant with the genes of an insect, or to cross a pig with a chicken. Plus, none of the tribesmen who selected the biggest, best ears of corn and wheat ever made proprietary claims on their "intellectual property," nor did they sue other tribesmen who dared save seed instead of buying it fresh every year from the "registered patent-holder."

Unfortunately, both of these scenarios are exactly what's at stake with genetic engineering, and the possible consequences will not easily be mitigated. The few extra pennies you spend on organic flour, and your appreciation of the difference it makes, are a boon and a prayer for the farmers struggling to make an honest living for themselves, an honest product for you, and a healthy environment for all of us and our children. They're working against daunting odds and big money.

WHY NOT 100% WHOLE WHEAT?

Bread made with white flour tends to "work" better because white flour has proportionally more gluten. Gluten has a star role in bread-making, and deserves an additional word: as a protein it is, by definition, a long "chain" molecule. It is also highly elastic. Like a rubber balloon, stretchy "nets" of gluten molecules trap the gases exhaled by yeasts, so loaves can rise and hold their shape. The same nets also provide a matrix for the molecules of starch in bread. The combination of starch and protein, when baked, creates the "crumb," or physical structure of the bread that makes possible such things as sliced bread and sandwiches.

Whole wheat flour has plenty of gluten, but also contains everything else in the original grain, including a large flake of indigestible bran. Bran absorbs water, lubricates your bowels, aids digestion, and cleanses your system. But it is also tough and fibrous and interferes with the development of good gluten webs. Whole grain flour also contains oils which can go rancid. Whole grain bread made with commercial yeast is generally crumbly, with poor keeping and slicing qualities. This may be partly due to the use of fats and sugars in baking, as well as the over-rapid fermentation of commercial yeasts.

Wonderful as it is to make light "artisan" style loaves, whole grain breads like desem (say "dayzum") or sprouted rye are worth learning to make. Both are the purest of the pure — nothing but whole grain, water, salt, and wild yeast. Whole

GLUTEN MOLECULES ARE LONG, KINKY CHAINS OF AMINO ACIDS — THE ATOMS THAT ATTRACT EACH OTHER, FORM THE KINKS...

KNEADING LOOSENS KINKS + ALIGNS THE CHAINS:

OVER-KNEADING BREAKS THE BONDS, DISSOLVES THE CHAINS + DESTROYS ELASTICITY...

AFTER AN ILLUSTRATION IN *ON FOOD & COOKING*, BY HAROLD MCGEE

CHAPTER THREE: SIMPLE SOURDOUGH BREAD

ISN'T WHITE FLOUR
"BAD" FOR YOU?
*Well, not necessarily. As
Harold McGee points
out, "Brown [whole
grain] bread contains
more nutrients than
white bread, but makes
it more difficult to
absorb them."* McGee
goes on to explain that
during World War II,
Irish citizens visibly
suffered when their diet
shifted from white to
whole wheat bread. (poor
U.S. Southerners for
whom whole corn was a
staple suffered a similar
malady called pellagra.)
In both instances, it
turns out processing
increases the availability
of certain essential
nutrients (though it
may decrease the overall
quantity of nutrients).
Likewise, the* natural
process of fermentation
also increases the
amount and variety of
nutrients available from
whole-grain sourdough.
**See McGee's
book,* On Food and
Cooking *— excellent
reading for
understanding bread
and other foods.*

rye flour gives a pungent and satisfying flavor to a wonderful, dense loaf that slices well and keeps for weeks, unrefrigerated, without going stale or moldy. And since it has little gluten, it requires little kneading. It does take longer to bake, and likes lots of steam and a lower temperature. In fact, if you have no oven, you can steam it on the stove top in about four hours. (People with severe gluten allergies should note that rye, barley, and oats all have some gluten, though not nearly so much as wheat.)

Desem is a wonderful exception to what most people know as "whole wheat" bread. It is by far one of the best and most wholesome breads around. It keeps well, and some say it's best on the third day after baking. Desem involves much the same process, with a few more tricks, including fresh-ground flour, careful shaping, proofing at high humidity and high temperature, and working your dough as wet as you can stand.

If you invest in a grain mill, you can buy bulk grains and grind your own flour. You can even make white flour by sifting out bran and germ through window screening — it may take several siftings — and aging your flour. (Unbleached white flour gets its lighter color from oxidation over time; some bakers say aged flour also improves the texture of the bread. Harold McGee can explain why.)

HOW IT WORKS — THE PROCESS IN DETAIL

I make bread by feel and by proportions, rather than by strict measurement, and that's not because I'm a pro (I'm not), but because I don't think and learn best "by doing," and it seems to me most others do too. It makes sense to me that learning is easier when we can use all our skills and senses. I think it also helps to get away from the notion of "doing it right the first time." If I never failed, I'd never learn. If you're hesitant, try working in small batches. Turn your failures into breakfast cereal, or bread crumbs, or compost. Get comfortable with the principles, and any recipe will be easier.

The three "tricks" are folded into the process here. Some people say waiting is another trick to good bread, since dough is sensitive to temperature and other environmental factors. But if you can plan to bake on a day when you'll be home, with good things to occupy you when you're not watching or working your dough, you'll start to catch the rhythm and it won't feel like waiting at all. It's like learning to dance with a new partner. You may feel clumsy 'til you get used to each other — so hold on, listen to the music, and keep moving your feet, so to speak.

STEP ONE: MAKE A "SPONGE."

The proportion of water determines everything else. Roughly, I figure about a cup per loaf. Using the same containers and bowls helps me keep track of my "recipe." Since I usually make fairly large batches, I often work with a quart yogurt container. If I want more bread and increase my water by half, I know roughly what to expect.

So I take my starter, about 1/4 to 1/2 cup, and add flour and water. The sponge should be wet, like batter for pancakes (cover it to keep out bugs and prevent drying). You make it wet because yeast will generally be livelier in a wet environment. They also like warmth (to a point; yeasts start to die at about 120 degrees F). You can adjust for cool conditions by increasing rising times and/or increasing water temperatures. Yeasts can accommodate a wide range of conditions; there's really no such thing as a "perfect" environment. Learn how dough responds in your kitchen, and figure out where and how you need to adjust.

The sponge ensures a yeast population strong enough to raise your dough in a reasonable amount of time. After your choice of flour, it is also where and how flavors get established in your dough. Generally, the wetter and warmer the sponge, and the longer you let it work, the more sour the dough.

STEP TWO: WAIT. LET YEASTS WORK & GROW SLOWLY.

Fermentation is naturally a slow process. Commercial yeast can speed it up, but does not necessarily make better bread. Indeed, the slow fermentation of natural sourdough makes wheat not only more digestible, but more nutritious — and better tasting, too! The rate of fermentation depends on temperature, altitude, humidity, and other environmental factors, including which yeasts are present (or not) in your area. Monitoring (and tasting) the process can teach you a lot about yeasts, and about bread.

As the yeasts grow and work on the flour, you'll notice that the sponge will become elastic, ropy and strong. It won't look like pancake batter any more — it will look stringy, sticky, and gooey — what they call a "ripe" starter in a bakery. That's your invitation to take the next step.

STEP THREE: SAVE A BIT OF SPONGE FOR "STARTER"

Your starter is a living thing! It transforms the combination of flour and water into something greater than the sum of the parts. Caring for it will make more sense as you begin to see and understand what it likes and needs, and how it performs under different conditions and with different flours (rye flour, for instance, is often used to liven up a sluggish sourdough).

Feed your starter to keep it strong. First, feed it immediately after you take it out of the sponge. Then feed it every week or so, either by making a fresh batch of bread, or by adding fresh flour and water. If you bake less than weekly, add dry flour to your starter until it makes a stiff dough. Stored in the fridge, it will hold for weeks, and even months — though it may take a while to get the starter back up to peak condition. Another suggestion that I haven't tried is to freeze your starter, which may require adjusting feeding and baking schedules accordingly.

Glass or ceramic is better for storing starter, as some plastics may react with alcohol, vinegar or other fermentation by-products. A loose lid can be important, as living yeasts produce more than enough carbon dioxide to explode a forgotten jar and make a mess of dough and broken glass in your fridge.

In the old days, starter was kept in a cool corner, or in the root cellar, and fed or used even every day. If you feed it frequently, you can use excess starter for sourdough pancakes or breakfast muffins (the sourness will improve the rising action of your baking soda). If you let it go a long time, it will start to smell vinegary. Too much sour can kill it, but before you toss a starter that's "gone," try perking it up with fresh water and flour. When in doubt, however, throw it out and start over. I have also dried starter and revived it, with good effect. If you forget to save unsalted starter, don't worry. Just take a bit of salted dough, break it up and dissolve it in a little water, and add flour. The salt will slow it down, but as you feed and use it, the salt and its effects will disappear.

STEP FOUR: ADD SALT & FLOUR TO YOUR SPONGE.

I figure about a teaspoon of salt per loaf (or per cup of water). Salt is important not just for flavor, but because it helps to condition and strengthen the dough, resulting in better rising and texture; it is also an important element in the critical equation of wet and warm versus cold and dry. On a cold day, you can encourage your dough by reducing salt, or holding it back until the last minutes of kneading (knead it right in, like flour — add just a little water if necessary. Taste the dough to make sure you're not too stingy with the salt.) To see how salt effects dough, try leaving it out of half your batch. Keep everything else the same, and compare.

Add flour and stir until you can't. Start kneading. Let it be sticky! It will smooth out as you knead. Rub dough off your hands and fingers with a bit of dry flour. But don't worry. As you knead, dough will start to stick to itself, and not your hands. Don't make it too dry! Yeasts don't like a desert environment, and though they won't go on strike, they may slow down. In fact, if the dough seems too sticky, try using water instead of flour. Kneading with water works well, and a wet, "loose" dough makes very different structure (lighter and more open) than a "stiff" dough. You might prefer it.

REVIVING A DYING STARTER
Yeasts (like humans?) will pollute their environment with their own wastes, which are acidic, and make them weak and sluggish. The best thing to do is to select a few brave pioneers and send them off to colonize a large, new virgin territory, with plenty of resources and no opposition. Try a teaspoon of old starter in 1/4-1/2 cup of fresh flour, with enough water to make a batter.

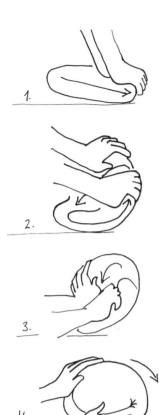

1.

2.

3.

4.

turn

ASW

KNEADING IS
EASIER FROM
ABOVE

STEP FIVE: KNEADING

"Vigorous" kneading means that you should break a sweat. The sweat does two things: First, it raises the temperature of the dough, which livens up the yeast. Second, as you knead, kinky strands of gluten lengthen, strengthen, and create a rubbery web that makes bread rise and gives it the structure, or "crumb" to survive slicing, buttering, and dunking in soup. You will see this vividly the first time you actually knead your dough for a full 15 minutes: it will go from a rough lump of sticky stuff that "tears" easily, to an elastic ball of moist, firm flesh as smooth and tight as the muscles of a conditioned athlete.

Kneading is great exercise for your arms and upper body! Let it be a wholesome discipline rather than an odious chore. It's less a matter of strength than rhythm. Knead to your favorite music! If you can only do it for a few minutes, the installment plan works too. Knead for four or five minutes. Let the dough rest for five to 20 minutes (or more) while you do something else. Repeat 'til done. (In professional bakeries, this is called the "autolyse" method, and includes withholding salt until the last, and allowing time for the dough to absorb more water. Without inhibitory salt, the yeast can better condition the gluten, reducing kneading time by nearly a third — which is a lot, when you're making hundreds of loaves.)

I find kneading much easier when I kneel on the ground or sit on my heels, with the dough in a big stainless steel bowl between my knees. I can use my full body weight easily, and as I fold and turn the dough, the bowl turns too. Flour stays in the bowl. (It is possible to over-knead, especially if you're making a small batch, so watch that clock — as you gain experience you'll feel when it's ready. If your dough suddenly starts to tear and go slack, you'll know you've over kneaded.)

STEP SIX: WAIT FOR THE BREAD TO RISE.

Faster bread is rarely better, though you can make it faster. I sometimes mix, knead, shape, proof, and bake. When it's warm from the oven, no one complains. But once you're used to the longer process, and you've worked it into the rhythm of your life, the total elapsed time won't be an issue. Mixing and kneading are a critical but brief benediction; the rest is between yeast, flour, water, and environment. You are judge.

Two risings, however, will make your loaves lighter, larger, tastier, and more healthful. (The sponge step is not considered a rising.) The rule of thumb is to let dough rise 'til it doubles in volume. This can take anywhere from one to six hours, depending on the dough, temperature, humidity, etc. If your dough is going faster than your oven, put it in a cooler spot, even in the fridge. If it's going slower, find it a warmer spot. Time things to suit yourself; bread is accommodating. But better too little heat than too much — you want the yeasts going into the oven strong so their last efforts aren't wasted!

The dough should also be covered with a clean cloth or piece of plastic (bag) to protect it from cooling drafts and keep it from drying out. You can rise dough in your kneading bowl or on a board. Buttering, while not necessary will keep it from sticking as it rises; butter, rather than oil, is less readily absorbed into the dough.

If you can remember what you did, how warm or cool it was, and how your bread felt and tasted, you can compare results with the next batch. Some bakers keep records of every aspect of every batch to better understand the reasons for particular failures and successes. A brewer friend of mine keep records, not for precision, but because "it is just my way of remembering and learning; a journal of my (bleary-eyed) travels…." Me, I like surprises. But however you go about it, you will invariably learn.

I light a fire in my oven at about this step in the process, but depending on your oven, the liveliness of your dough, and your schedule, you may want to light yours earlier. Better to have the oven waiting for the bread than the bread waiting for the oven, so when in doubt, light your fire early.

STEP SEVEN: SHAPE YOUR LOAVES

Divide your dough into as many lumps as you want loaves. Shape the lumps gently into loaves, being careful not to tear the gluten "skin." Gently fold and press out big air bubbles 'til the dough feels firm. Many bakers break up the shaping into two stages with a few minutes rest in between because it makes better, higher rising loaves. After shaping, set your loaves in a warm or cool spot as needed.

BEAUTIFUL LOAVES

You can make loaves of any shape — try traditional braided rings, or fanciful figures like the luscious mermaids my mother used to make. Dough will stick to just about anything, so grease pans and trays, or dust boards and baskets with liberal amounts of flour. Traditional cloth-lined or wicker baskets make beautiful loaves because the dough picks up the pattern of the weaving (and that becomes the top of the loaf).

STEP EIGHT: "PROOF" YOUR LOAVES

"Proofing" isn't a precise science. When the loaves have risen to near double size, they are ready to bake. See how the dough responds when you poke it with a finger (gently). It should be soft and impressionable, but still have some spring. If you're not sure, better to bake than wait.

STEP NINE: BAKE

If you're using a peel to load your oven, dust the surface with corn meal, to help the loaves slide off easily. Slash the surface of the dough with a knife (very sharp or serrated), or use a razor blade. Hold your blade at about 45 degrees, and make a slash about 1/2 inch deep, in whatever design pleases you (when Canadian families baked in communal ovens, each family had their own "brand" so they knew which loaves were theirs). Place the peel in the oven where you want the loaf to end up, and flick the peel out from under.

Just as the secret to a firm, chewy crumb is in the kneading, the secret to crusts is superheated steam, which caramelizes sugars in the crust, producing the hard, shiny, golden brown surface prized by bread-lovers. (Less steam makes a drier, thicker crust.) Steam also improves "oven spring," the last surge of yeasty activity that makes the loaves puff up high. Steam does this by briefly cooling the oven, keeping the surface of the dough soft and elastic and giving the yeasts a bit more time in which to work before the heat does them in.

An oven full of bread will steam itself, as each pound of dough produces a couple of ounces of steam. However, if your oven is half full, you can add steam or hot water. The first ten minutes is when you need it. Professional bakeries use preheated, pressurized steam jets because they don't want to

PULLING THE REMAINS OF THE FIRE
Note the metal barrel at lower right — a Weber-type grill also makes a good receptacle for hot coals, and you can use it to grill burgers while you wait for hot bread.
(D. Lesley photo)

cool the oven. They also try to avoid getting water on the bricks themselves, as the sudden temperature shock can damage bricks and bring sand boiling up from underneath. I have had good success punching a small hole in a tin can and filling it with (hot) water so it leaks gradually — best done on a cookie sheet already preheated and waiting in the oven. You might also try a (clean) spray bottle, or a spray nozzle on your hose. The finer (and hotter) the spray the better. Be careful in a small oven not to introduce too much water too fast.

Your nose (or your intuition) will tell you when your bread is ready. The loaves will call you to the oven. If it smells right, take a peek (beware waves of heat or steam when opening the door). Tap the loaves on the bottom. If they sound hollow, they're done. If they don't, they may need more time, even if they seem quite dark. Heavier dough with more whole grain flour will take longer.

Cooking is a function of time and temperature. Increase one, and decrease the other. Baking time in a mud oven can range from 20-60 minutes or more, depending on your oven temperature and the kind of bread. Bread steams beautifully in about four hours on a stove top at 212 degrees. But no matter what, bread is done when the center of the loaf reaches 190° to 200°, at least.

STEP TEN: WAIT

Don't eat — yet — the bread is still cooking! The center may have just reached cooking temperatures. Cut it, and it will cool instead of finishing its bake. In 20 minutes, however, it will be thoroughly done, and still warm enough to melt your butter!

LOADING THE LOAVES
(D. Lesley photo)

SCREENING DIRT

If you have a lot of material to screen, it's worth setting up a frame like this, with legs to hold it at the right angle. If all you can get is 1/2 inch hardware cloth, screen out smaller stuff by setting it at a higher angle. (H. Field, photo)

BUILD YOUR OWN EARTH OVEN

CHAPTER FOUR:
MATERIALS & MAKING DO

Building something by yourself and for yourself is less about following instructions than it is about paying attention to where you are and what you're doing. It's about making the most of your materials — accepting and cooperating with their limits, rather than forcing them to work against their nature. It's a basic working principle that applies to mud or people. And there's a corollary: where we find relationship, we will also find beauty. But we have to start where we are. That's why I suggest you make do — not because it's better than buying, but because you'll learn more by thinking about where to dig and how to scrounge. Yes, most of the industrialized world is a consumer culture, but we are a minority! The reality is that consumption does not (and cannot) sustain human culture. Everything comes from and returns to the earth. Buying encourages us to forget that. Scrounging and recycling reminds us that there is no such thing as "waste," only gifts we fail to cherish.

A few years ago, a national home and garden magazine revisited one of their most popular projects — an "adobe" oven. The oven was practical and attractive — but not cheap or simple. The materials list included 28 concrete blocks, 68 firebricks, wire mesh, chicken wire, fancy deck screws, aluminum flashing, three hundred pounds of cement, about a ton of "adobe soil," and latex paint — well over a hundred dollars worth. Not much for a nine to five professional, but a good week's expenses for a subsistence artist!

If you're feeling rushed and buying is the only way you can save time, why not let the oven wait? "There is more to life than increasing its speed." Try a one-day, one-layer oven on sawhorses (see Chapter Five). It can be a practice oven, as temporary or as permanent as you like. Take the time you save to inventory local resources. Try different routes to work and look for materials at construction sites, giveaway piles, or vacant lots. Buy good bread and ask bakers about their oven (see if they don't get excited when they hear about your wood-fired oven plans). By the time you figure out how and where to make a more permanent oven, you'll not only have located all the right stuff, you'll have perfected your bread, too!

And finally, this chapter also talks about some sophisticated and more expensive materials, because sometimes that's what you need.

FLOOR MATERIALS
(TILE, SOAPSTONE, MUD, ETC.)

- Mexican tile: unglazed ceramic floor tile is often available cheap or free from vendors who sometimes buy more than they need. Harder tile is not necessarily more durable, and may be brittle and less resistant to the rapid heating and cooling cycles in an oven; look for thick, low-fired varieties.
- Stone is not recommended for floors, unless you can find soapstone (look for old, broken soapstone sinks). Even soapstone, however, should be dried slowly and heated carefully, otherwise moisture pockets can develop tremendous explosive pressure, destroying your floor and possibly causing you bodily harm. It may also hold more heat than you need. For that reason, it is sometimes used as a subfloor.
- Plain subsoil will make a floor, and can be fired hard. (Mexican tile is, in fact, usually made of local, silty clay soil deposits.) I haven't tested this one myself, but would advise against mixing in any sand, due to different expansion and contraction rate. I might also make the clay-soil first into tiles, mixing it with water and working it until it's plastic like modeling clay, then rolling out tiles and setting them on a layer of dry sand, so that they can move as they shrink. I might also pre-fire the tiles, if possible. Then I would lay the oven floor and build the oven.)
- Another suggestion, if you're in the mood for experiments, is "an old European oven floor recipe" made of lime putty, wood ash, and sand. Try starting with a mix of one part lime, 1/2 part ash, and 3 parts sand, and experimenting from there. A Spaniard reported seeing it used in Majorca. (See the Lime plaster section on page 76 for more info on this traditional material.)

STRAW & OTHER FIBERS

Straw is often treated as "waste." Grass farmers in the Willamette valley near where I live used to burn all the straw left on their fields after harvest. Immense stacks of huge bales are often left to rot. In most other places as well, straw is fairly cheap. Try feed stores, stables, or a farmer. Hay is generally more expensive because it contains grass leaves and stalks, complete with seed head, which provide nutrition for the livestock. However, at the end of a mild winter, many horse or cattle owners may have old hay they no longer want. Ask!

Any reasonably tough vegetable fiber will work. Long grass from your yard, cattail fluff, old rags or sisal rope chopped short and shredded, sawdust, or dry leaves might work — when in doubt, try it! If you're making cob or plaster, you want some length to give the material plasticity and tensile strength. (If you're making insulation, it doesn't matter how short the fibers are, but it does matter that they not compress too easily; cattail fluff, for example, would pack down too much to make insulation.)

Don't use synthetics — natural materials subjected to high heat will burn out, leaving only carbon and (insulative) air spaces. Synthetics will melt and fuse into a nasty mess, producing toxic fumes as well.

GRAVEL & SAND

A sand or gravel pit is just an old river bed that the river has abandoned. There may be a place you can dig for free, such as a sand bar. In general, you want to stay away from beach sand because it tends to be rounded and smooth Sometimes you can dig in old pits that are no longer commercially viable but that still have plenty of material. (You may need permission from land owners and/or state or federal authorities.) Working quarries sell a sandy kind of gravel (often called something like "quarter minus," because it's what falls through a quarter-inch screen). It's also worth asking if they have any waste material to give away, like crusher "fines" (the stuff too small to use for gravel), or "scalpings" (dirty gravel that is scraped off the top of the rock pit). If you want the pleasure of mixing mud with bare feet, though, beware sharp-edged gravel that chews on tender toes!

SUBSOIL, CLAY, &
WHAT TO DO IF YOU CAN'T FIND IT

You can build with just about any clay soil underfoot. Most subsoils should have clay enough to be sticky. The best test is experience. Try it out, and see what works.

If your soil has clay, but not enough to make cob, you can purify it to increase clay content. Let it dry, pulverize it as fine as you can, screen out rocks, and soak the rest in water. Mix it up to suspend the clay. Let the sand settle anywhere from a few seconds up to up to 30 minutes. (Longer settling means purer clay.) Your water should still look cloudy with clay. Pour it off into another bucket, and let it settle *again*. When the water clears, pout it off, let the clay dry, and see how it works.

There are places where clay subsoil is either rare or hard to harvest, including desert areas where the geology is mostly volcanic, some coastal regions, and cities where it's just plain hard to find clean soil. If that's where you live, you still have options: Take a long drive and look in road cuts or excavation sites. Find a geologist (at a local university or a branch of the US Geological Survey) and ask where to look for clay. Find a potter or a local college ceramics department that's too busy to recycle their waste clay, and ask for some. (You may have to soak it, dry it, work it, or all three, but the price should be right. Be aware that potter's clay is much purer stuff. If you use it to make cob, you may need as little as five to ten percent to make a good, sticky mix; certainly no more than 20%.)

Or buy mason's "fireclay" from a building supplier. Masons mix it with cement and sand to make mortar; it comes dry and powdered in 50 pound bags.

CLAY FACTS

RESOURCE
William Bryant Logan assembled these facts in a marvelous book of essays titled, Dirt, The Ecstatic Skin of the Earth.

The Bible says we're made of clay ("Adam" is Hebrew for "red clay"). That may be because it is perhaps the most common and widespread substance on earth, but some scientists also hypothesize that life actually originated in a "soup" of clay, water, organic compounds, and energy from light or lightning. In addition, the crystalline structure of clays exhibit a logic of coding similar to DNA, the building block of life. And of all earthly phenomena, only two require water for their existence: clay, and life. It is estimated that all the clay on the planet, evenly spread out, would make a layer a mile thick — which is not surprising, given that clay is decomposed rock.

What distinguishes clay from other dirt is particle size, as well as molecular and chemical properties. Size is very important: a grain of coarse sand falls through four inches of water in one second, a grain of silt takes five minutes, and a single grain of very fine clay can take up to 860 years! Clay is so slow partly because of shape as well as size — particles are thin and flat. Indeed, a single gram of clay can have a surface area larger than a football field. That flatness helps make clay plastic — flat surfaces make it easy for particles to stick, like two wet sheets of paper. In addition to size and shape, however, clay particles are also electrically charged, which means that they have a tremendous capacity to attract and adhere to clay or other molecules (including water). All these properties make clay the wonderful, magical substance that it is.

REFRACTORY CEMENT

If you're going to be baking a lot, you might want an inner thermal shell made of something a bit tougher than clay, to withstand regular gouging, poking, and heavy usage. Regular Portland cement, however, is not a good option. Even at the relatively low temperatures of a bread oven, it breaks down and loses strength. Brick is an excellent choice, but making a brick oven is quite a bit more complicated than making one out of mud.

A relatively simple alternative to brick is high temperature refractory cement. Refractory cements are specially formulated to withstand high heat. Mixed with sand, you can mold it over a sand form like mud (although you'll need to use rubber gloves to protect your hands, since it's a caustic material).

If you decide to use refractory cement, you might want to do some research, since things like reinforcement and expansion cracking are different than they are with regular portland cement. I did use chicken wire to reinforce my mobile pizza oven, and it seems to be holding up, but I have been advised that metal reinforcement in a refractory cement may be counterproductive. Many manufacturers have technicians who can answer questions and offer guidance over the phone. There are many different makes available, so it's worth calling around to see what's available near you at what price. The product I've used with good success is a calcium-aluminate cement sold by:

LaFarge Calcium Aluminates
9033 Laurel Branch Circle
Mechanicsville, VA 23111
1800-524-8463

ABOUT CEMENT
Clay and rock, cooked at very high temperature, ground into powder and mixed to carefully engineered proportions become modern "hydraulic cement." On mixing with water it undergoes a chemical reaction to become hard, rocklike, and impervious to water. It will also set up and harden under water. When you mix cement with sand and gravel, it binds everything together into concrete. The chemical composition of the source clay and rock is what determines heat resistance.

A SMALL, ONE-DAY OVEN:
The floor is only five bricks deep, and two and a half wide, yet we could make small pizza in it! The shape is also longer than wide, because that's all we could do with the bricks we had.

HELP! NO SAND:
But plenty of topsoil, as this was in Minnesota, where the ancient floodplain of the Mississippi laid down topsoil tens of feet deep. A layer of newspaper would have helped when it was time to pull the form, but I didn't think of it. Since I also had no straw, I just decided to try making it out of pure clay subsoil, which I found in a nearby hillside. I fired it dry the next day, ready for baking!

CHAPTER FIVE; OTHER MIXTURES, OTHER OVENS

SINGLE LAYER, ALL-CLAY, "RAMMED EARTH" OVENS

The absolute simplest oven I've made was a half day demonstration oven I did a couple years ago for a weekend festival. I was visiting my father and second mother during a biannual "meadow fest" at their pottery works. They provide homemade snacks and great bread, so I offered to make a small, temporary pizza oven. The foundation was a couple of stout planks on saw horses. On top, I set a layer of old, four inch thick concrete pavers, a layer of sand, and a firebrick floor. (Such a thin subfloor didn't seem unsafe, since it was a very small oven. For a larger one, I would have wanted more distance and material — preferably insulation — between wood and fire. See the section below on insulation.)

I made the form of top soil, because I didn't have enough sand. The oven itself was a single thick layer of clayey subsoil, dug straight out of the hillside. Since the clay was moist from the ground (but not wet), I could pack it directly around the form in a layer four to five inches thick. Then I took a piece of 2x4 and whacked it, hard, all around, until the material was solid and smooth. I cut a door, lit a fire in the oven, and we were eating pizza out of it the next day! (It did crack, quite a bit, but I just filled the cracks from the outside, and didn't worry.) A year or more later, it's still in perfect shape, and this was under a tarp, after a Minnesota winter! The pizza was such a hit that they're talking about making a bigger and more permanent oven.

This one convinced me of the benefits of a pure clay thermal layer. While a sand-clay mix is denser than pure clay subsoil and able to store more heat, sand can cause problems. Fire fuses or "bisques" the inner inch or so of clay into a hard, integral mass. Sand requires much more heat for fusing, so it just expands and contracts — at a different rate than clay.

ALMOST READY FOR BAKING!

As a result, sand grains may fall out of the clay, and if you don't scuffle the floor perfectly, you can get sand in your bottom crusts. Clay can crack and spall too, but even when bisque-fired, it's usually softer, less sandy, and less likely to break a tooth.

The "all-clay" ovens I've made have used homogenous clay subsoils, with lots of silt, but no sand (the silt helps minimize shrinkage — but Quebec ovens were apparently made of purer stuff, and held up fine). Whatever you find to use, when you pack it around the sand form, it should be malleable enough to make a hard, solid ball in your hand, but shouldn't be so soft as to squish between your fingers when you squeeze. That way, when you tamp it, it will compact and become solid and hard, instead of splooging out sideways. (Test for water content with a snowball test: dropped on a hard surface from chest high, it should hold together without breaking apart, but not be so wet that it loses its ball shape.)

SIMPLER FOUNDATIONS

A foundation doesn't need to last 1,000 years. On a practical level, all it does is keep an oven off the wet ground and bring it up to a good working height. If rock or concrete is more than you want to deal with, sawhorses and stout planks will do. So will plastic five-gallon buckets, wood boxes, railroad ties, logs, tires filled with sand or earth, or wire fencing filled with rubble. Use your imagination and whatever you can find. (If you do make a wood base, please read the section on insulating oven floors. If you're not careful, it's easy to burn one out!)

If you want a permanent foundation, but don't have material to make it as high as you want it, make it low. Lay a single course of water-resistant stuff to ensure a capillary break against rising ground moisture, and build the rest of your foundation with cob. (Just make sure the cob is strong and dry enough before you fill and/or build on it.)

SCULPTING & FINISHING

Sculpture is everywhere — in plants, in animals, in the implements we use every day, in fruits and vegetables, as well as in books of ancient and modern arts. If you want to sculpt your oven, you've probably already started, and are just reading this because it's gotten too dark to work outside. I'm assuming you've already read the section on finishing plasters, which is what you'll need for sculptural details. So. Here are some other ideas:

Build up rough forms directly on the oven using the wetter cob mix with straw. Or make models of cob, to see what pleases you and to work out your ideas in three dimensions. Both ways have their merits. As your form becomes more defined, use a finer plaster with shorter straw and maybe even with finer sand — much easier to sculpt, mold, and finish.

Keep in mind that there are limits to what shapes wet mud will hold without reinforcement — and reinforce as needed. If your sculpture extends so far out from the main form that it starts to tear away and fall, knead long straw into the cob to make "straps" and use them like thick tape to tie things together. You can also imbed bits of wood in the mud as anchors or "deadmen." Before you bury it in the mud though, tie it with a piece of natural fiber string or wire. When it is well anchored under heavy cob, use the string to wrap hanging parts of the form. You can also use cloth or sticks in a similar way, or use your imagination in new ways! (See photos, page 81.)

The right tools will also help you define and refine shapes and sculptural lines. Spoons and knives are high on my list, but try whatever you have: kitchen utensils, masonry trowels, sticks, stones, etc. Small sticks with cut or broken ends can make wonderful surface patterns and texture, and you can also inlay things into the mud itself: bits of tile, wood, stone, glass, ceramic, what-have-you.

TWO TIPS
1. Stand back! You can't make sense of the whole unless you can see it, and you can't see it if you're 12 inches away. Get a new, more complete perspective.
2. Every shape is made of flat planes. Curved planes are just many small flat planes smoothed together. Establish large planes with a flat board, or trowel, or with a knife. As you work, you'll see how the planes are connected.

LIME PLASTERS & OTHER WATER-RESISTANT, BREATHABLE PLASTERS; AND A WARNING

Lime plasters are traditionally used to protect earthen houses against weather, even in grey, rainy England! Lime plaster makes a beautiful, water-resistant surface, is lovely to use, and takes color well (Michelangelo's Sistine ceiling and Diego Rivera's murals were painted on lime plaster, and many of their pigments were made from colored local soils).

Lime is best made into a "putty," which you can approximate by soaking standard mason's lime in water. Like cement, lime is caustic and should be handled with care and/ or rubber gloves and eye protection. The fresher you can buy your lime, the better, as it "goes off" and loses effectiveness with exposure to moisture in the air. Lime putty will keep as long as it's wet. Freezing improves it, but old, stiff putty is tough to break up and mix with sand. Whip it up with an electric drill with a steel paint mixing blade. Or push the putty through a fine screen.

Basic lime plasters are made of three parts sand to one part lime putty (not powdered stuff). In practice, proportions can vary, but the principle is much as it is for clay-sand mixes: the more lime, the more cracking you can expect. Add fiber if you can — it will help hold everything together, especially if you're putting on a thick undercoat. Horsehair is traditional, but chopped straw or manure work too.

Litema (pronounced "dee-TAY-ma") is an African plaster made of pure manure and clay. It is lovely to work with. On an oven or building, the first fine layer of clay washes off, leaving a layer of impressively tough fibers that shed water, much like a thatch roof. It is not waterproof (nor would you want it to be) but it will limit water absorption.

Materials are easy enough to collect. If you find colored clays, litema is a great vehicle for applying them in decorative ways. As for manure, cows (with their many stomachs) produce a finer material than horses, and fresh stuff is better than old dry lumps (people have suggested that various live enzymes make it stickier). However, if you're worried about e. coli or salmonella (both real possibilities), or if you're squeamish about working with fresh manure and can't find your rubber gloves, dry manure responds well to soaking in water or grating on a piece of 1/4 inch hardware cloth.

JASON'S OVEN AFTER
A HARD WINTER
*note the beautifully
molded door and
handles, which were
shaped out of lump of
straw-ey cob and
cement (for more on
molded cob doors, see
page 83).*

THE WARNING

Builders I know tell me of uncovered ovens holding up with
no more protection from the weather than a layer of litema.
I've seen pictures of the ovens, which look fine, but I doubt
they're dry enough to bake in without a very long firing. And
given a rainy day, which would you choose, an oven under a
roof, or one under a rain cloud?

My friend Jason made a beautiful oven that sits in a lovely
glade near his straw bale "dirt yurt." He didn't want to hide
the lovely shape of the oven, so he finished it with the same
lime plaster that he used on his bale walls. It hardened well,
but the oven, with a top horizontal surface exposed, soaked up
lots of water; the plaster cracked and fell off, and the oven
started to deteriorate. It came back to life with a new coat of
plaster, but in a harsher climate with more freezing, the
damage would have been worse. The plaster on the bale walls
is fine, and I think it would have been fine on the oven if
somehow the flat top surface could have been made to shed
water — maybe even with just a "Chinaman's hat" of tin on
top, or a pitched piece of flagstone.

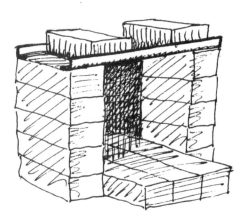

AN EASY-TO-MAKE "FLAT" ARCH
Angle iron or other metal supports between columns of stacked bricks — no mortar needed, and if you're building a chimney, just leave out the middle brick.

BRICK OR METAL DOORWAYS

The doorway is the most vulnerable area of the oven. If you're gentle and careful when you bake, a cob doorway will last a long time. But if you tend to bang or poke it a lot, or you're doing production baking, or dealing with kids, you might want to consider making a more durable doorway of brick or metal.

A brick arch is easy enough. Use plain red brick. Lay them out on the ground to get a sense of what the arch should look like, and what kind of spacing you'll need between the bricks. Make a form of sand or plywood, and use fine sand and clay for mortar. Or simply make two vertical doorjambs of stacked bricks, and span the top with a piece of angle iron or other heavy scrap metal. If you want really nice traditional metal oven doors such as were used on Canadian clay ovens, contact Ovencrafters in California (see Resources).

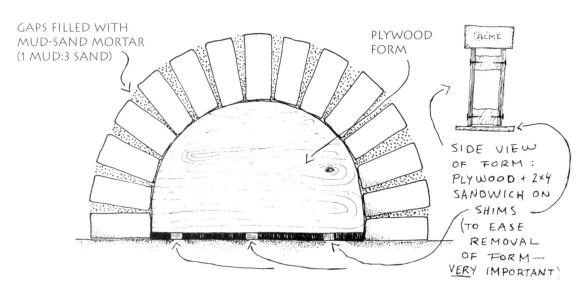

GAPS FILLED WITH MUD-SAND MORTAR (1 MUD:3 SAND)

PLYWOOD FORM

SIDE VIEW OF FORM: PLYWOOD + 2×4 SANDWICH ON SHIMS (TO EASE REMOVAL OF FORM — VERY IMPORTANT)

A FANCIER, MORE CLASSICAL ARCH, BUT REALLY NOT THAT MUCH HARDER TO BUILD.

BUILD YOUR OWN EARTH OVEN

CHIMNEYS & DOORS: FOR CONVENIENCE, WIND PROTECTION, AND EFFICIENCY

A chimney can do several things for your oven: it can improve draft; it can help get smoke out of your way; and depending on your oven, it can increase efficiency (how much depends on how you make your door, but more on that later.) Efficiency aside, however, when working the fire or cooking pizza, it can make all the difference to have the smoke out of your face. And if you're sculpting an animal oven, chimneys add drama by giving your beast a breath of fire!

If you've already built your oven but decided you really need a chimney, you can easily add one on. You could just poke a hole in the top of your oven dome — it would definitely get the smoke out of your way. However, most of the heat would go with it. Heat from the fire would travel a short, direct path from point of combustion to point of escape. What you want is to keep the heat in the oven as long as possible before letting it out. So, better than poking a hole in the top of your oven, design it so that oxygen, smoke, and flame all swirl around in the oven as long as possible before they leave.

In fact, the basic oven shape is already close to a fairly sophisticated "downdraft" design. Oxygen comes in the bottom of the door, sweeps across and through the fire, rises up with the heat of combustion to roll against the oven roof, and finally sweeps down again and out the top of the door. In a well-burning oven, the rolling, up-and-down movement of the fire is plain to see.

But the smoke may linger, and the wind can blow back into the door, choking the fire and making it burn poorly. Just holding a tube or section of stove pipe over the top of the door will draw away smoke, and probably improve the burn. So the logical first choice for a chimney is to build out the sides of the doorway to support a piece of stovepipe, or a cob chimney right over the top of the oven door.

NOTE THE CUSTOM-MADE, WELDED STEEL DOORFRAME AND CHIMNEY
The rock is leaning against a piece of cardboard, which is keeping the sand form from falling out of the open door (photo courtesy of N. Waddoups)

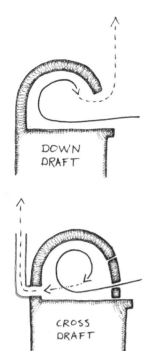

DOWN
DRAFT

CROSS
DRAFT

You can also build a chimney at the back of the oven, creating a "cross-draft" design that works much like the down-draft. With the chimney opening just an inch or two above floor level and directly across from the door, air enters the fire, rolls up and over the top of the oven, comes back down (helping to preheat incoming air), and sweeps across the floor again prior to heading out the chimney.

Either way, a chimney gives you greater, and more precise control over how much oxygen gets to the fire, and how fast. By partially closing the doorway in front of the chimney, so the air has to rush in through cracks and holes, the fire will burn brighter. (For a brief discussion of why this is so, see Chapter Six on the "mechanics of fire.")

A suggested guideline is to make the chimney 1/4 to 1/5 the diameter of the oven chamber (five to seven inches for a 27 inch diameter oven), but experiment with various tubes to see what works best for you. Try rolled up sheet metal roofing, sections of old metal chimney, etc.

To construct the actual chimney, mold cob into snakes. Coil the snakes around and up, like making a pot. Or set a piece of clay tile, cement, or tin pipe into the cob. Or use a series of tin cans with the ends cut out as forms to pack cob around. Place them end-to-end and don't worry about joining them; the cob will seal any gaps. Cardboard tubing will serve the purpose, and burn out upon firing (be advised, however, that smoldering paper that doesn't burn out quickly can also char and curl up, blocking off your chimney — the longer or more curved the chimney, the worse the problem). You can also make a removable chimney from an old piece of tin pipe or roofing cut and bent to stand on the hearth and fit close around the doorway. Keep your chimney as straight as possible, because every bend will drastically decrease its effectiveness.

USING A DEADMAN: Note the wire under the hand. It's attached to a piece of wood buried in the cob, and at the other end, it's keeping the cardboard tube from tipping over with the weight of the wet mud. (photo courtesy of N. Waddoups)

USING STRING TO HOLD A WET COB CHIMNEY IN PLACE FOR DRYING: Wet cob on a slightly out-of-plumb chimney would fall off due to it's own weight. Wrapping the wet cob with string holds it 'til dry. Rags soaked in clay slip also work. (photo courtesy of N. Waddoups)

FIRING DOORS

Chimneys complicate door-making. In a chimney-less oven, when the door is shut, nothing goes in or out. When you add a chimney, you're effectively adding a second door. Covering the mouth of the oven isn't enough; you have to be able to close the chimney too. In addition, when you add a chimney, you change how the fire burns.

An oven with a chimney will burn just fine without a firing door, but it's worth learning how air flow can affect your fire. A firing door allows you to have greater control over air flow. A tight fit isn't crucial. In fact, you may need to cut vents in a metal door to ensure that the fire gets adequate air. But remember that any metal will get very hot, so put some kind of insulating material between the handle and the door itself.

With a rear chimney, you'll need to devise a separate damper to close it off. This should be as close to the oven as possible, or even inside the oven, to minimize radiant surfaces that will suck out heat.

Remember that when you close the oven up to let it "soak," it will probably be hot enough to char a wooden door. You can prevent this by soaking the door in water, or by protecting its inner surface with metal and/or insulation.

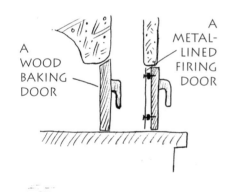

A WOOD BAKING DOOR

A METAL-LINED FIRING DOOR

If you build a chimney in front, you can build it out from the door so that when you close off the oven, you've closed off the chimney too. Make sure your chimney support structure is big enough to allow you to maneuver your baking door in and out. You may want to make a metal firing door that will allow you to better control airflow into the fire. In a pinch, however, a sheet of tin will work. You can also make a thick door of cob and straw to serve as both baking and firing door (see illustrations).

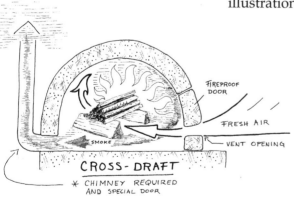

CROSS-DRAFT

FIREPROOF DOOR

FRESH AIR

SMOKE

VENT OPENING

* CHIMNEY REQUIRED AND SPECIAL DOOR

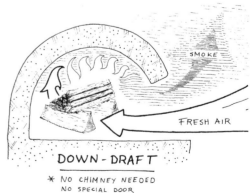

DOWN-DRAFT

SMOKE

FRESH AIR

* NO CHIMNEY NEEDED NO SPECIAL DOOR

BUILD YOUR OWN EARTH OVEN

THE HOLE IN THE DOOR ALSO MAKES A PLACE TO INSERT A STICK FOR A HANDLE

IN THIS POSITION, A COB DOOR ALLOWS AIR TO GET TO THE FIRE, AND SMOKE TO GO UP THE CHIMNEY.

CLOSED OFF WITH A PLUG & PUSHED FURTHER IN, THE SAME DOOR SEALS THE OVEN FOR BAKING.

COB DOORS

It is easy to make a very simple and practical door of cob. After you've cut open the oven and smoothed the edges of the doorway (easier after it's dry), mix a lump of wet, very straw-ey cob into a shape that fits snugly in the opening; make it thick enough to hold together and to hold heat. Also make sure that your doorway is shaped to allow the cob door to both block off the chimney (for baking) and let smoke escape up the chimney (for firing). Use a stick or finger to make a generous hole all the way through the door. The hole will provide air for the fire, and a place where you can insert a stick handle to remove the door when hot. Make a cob plug to seal the hole when baking. If you want to make a more durable door, add some cement to the mix. Remember that cement is caustic; use caution and/or rubber gloves.

INSULATING A MUD OVEN

As most people who pay for heating fuel are aware, insulation is crucial for increasing efficiency. In a high mass, masonry style oven, most of the energy goes into getting the mass hot. Once the mass has absorbed enough heat, it doesn't take nearly as much to *keep* it hot. Because insulation performs the opposite function of thermal mass, it has to be a light, loose material that *doesn't* absorb heat and will keep it from moving *out*. More thickness = better insulation. So commercial bakeries with big brick ovens will often blanket them with a foot or more of heat resistant insulating material. Some can maintain baking temperatures for *days!*

Most small mud ovens for home use probably don't need it, but you might decide otherwise, especially if you're baking in very cold weather, or doing a lot of baking over extended periods of time. I'm providing the following information as a starting place, since insulating mud ovens, especially with straw clay, is a fairly recent phenomenon (so far as I know).

AN INSULATING MATTRESS *UNDER* YOUR OVEN

The heat of the fire will be conducted through the floor bricks to what's underneath. Dense, conductive materials like sand, rock, and rubble not only store heat for baking, but they also suck it out of a hot oven. (Remember, heat only rises in a gas or fluid — in a conductive material like brick or sand it will go all directions.) This is perhaps of greatest concern under the oven, which may sit on a few feet of rock and sand.

You can insulate your oven floor with a few dollars worth of perlite, pumice, or vermiculite, which are mineral insulators that can support quite a bit of weight (more about what they are and where to get them on the next page). But give yourself at least four inches of sand under your firebrick — more if it's a big oven, or if you want to be able to bake over extended periods — and then four to 12 inches of insulation. Keep your sand from drifting down into the perlite by separating it with a thin layer of cob.

If you make a base of wood, you'll need enough mass (sand) or insulation to protect the wood from heat that will be transferred downwards through conductive materials to the wood, which will char and eventually burn through (I've had it happen!) The amount of sand or insulation may vary, depending on the size of the oven, how long you fire it, and what you use for a floor. To protect a wooden base under an oven two and a half to three feet in diameter, with a firebrick floor two and a half inches thick, I would want at least four to six inches of sand, plus two inches of insulation, for good measure. I have gotten away with no insulation, and about two to three inches of sand, but that was a soapstone floor, and the wood did char…. If you take risks, be careful and make contingencies in case of failure.

PUMICE, PERLITE, OR VERMICULITE

These materials are basically rock that has been expanded or "puffed" at high temperature — not unlike "puffed wheat" cereal, or popcorn. As such, they are not only lightweight and heat-resistant, but still strong enough to support weight. (Fiberglass may be excellent insulation, but it has no compressive strength to support weight. It is also a nasty material to mix with something as friendly as mud.) The others are easy to mix with clay or high-temperature cement as needed to make various shapes and forms.

Pumice, of course, is naturally occurring, made when volcanoes spew highly pressurized, molten rock into a cooler atmosphere. Perlite and vermiculite are man-made, and their manufacture requires large amounts of energy. Given that all three must be mined, using pumice probably makes the most sense environmentally, unless you live very far from the source. Your building or landscape supplier is likely to be the cheapest source, but failing that, try a garden supply store or a large nursery that makes its own potting soil — they're more likely to be able to sell in bulk, rather than expensive little bags.

AN INSULATING
BLANKET *OVER* YOUR OVEN

Insulation Improvements
This is the 5th printing and I've switched to insulating with coarse sawdust-chainsaw leavings, planer shavings, "bark dust," etc. (Fine sawdust works, but holds more water which can soak into the layer below, causing slumping. If you use it, best to apply it on a dry first layer.) I mix it in a wheelbarrow with clay slip and toss until uniform. It should pack well so you can work it around the oven like a layer of mud 2-6" thick.
Our household oven, which we use every 1 or 2 weeks, has a 4-5" dense layer (no straw), about 6" of insulation, and about 1" of finish plaster. It holds cooking temps for 6-12 hours easy.

A few years ago we started insulating ovens with a natural building material that has been used in Europe for centuries. Known as straw-clay, or light-clay, it is simply loose straw coated with clay slip and compacted. In Europe, it was traditionally used to fill the gaps in timber-frame walls. Compacted into removable wooden frames, it is both fireproof and insulative.

If you're considering insulating, see how your oven works without it. You can always add it later. Straw clay is a pretty good insulator, but it's not that light. Perlite or vermiculite might be better choices for an oft-used oven. You can mix them with clay slip as you would straw, but that would reduce their insulation value somewhat. The best option for insulating might be to build an exterior shell of thin cob, and fill the space with loose perlite.

MAKING STRAW-CLAY

"Slip" is how you coat your straw with an even, light layer of clay. You make slip by mixing clay and water until the clay is evenly dispersed and suspended. It should not settle out in an hour. (If it does, you may need to find purer, finer stuff.) Work out lumps until they disperse. An electric drill with a paint-mixing attachment helps, or you can push it through window screening or a big kitchen sieve, or smoosh it around with your feet on tarp or pavement until it goes liquid. Or dry your clay and pound it into a fine powder prior to soaking it. *(Don't breathe dry clay dust!)* Do whatever works until it's a bit thicker than heavy cream and coats your hand with an opaque film of liquid clay. You'll need several five-gallon buckets full, depending on how thick you insulate.

Now break up some straw in a wheelbarrow, on a sheet of plywood, or on any other hard surface. Pour slip over the straw and toss lightly, just like dressing a salad. A hay fork makes it easier, but hands work fine. Everything should be evenly coated. Take a handful and wring it like a wet towel. Liquid clay should ooze (not stream) out of the straw. Adjust proportions as needed.

A HALF-INSULATED OVEN
Note the stone foundation with a partial floor of wood, which created firewood storage underneath. It burnt through because I didn't use enough insulation under the floor! It does, however, sit very safely on a concrete pad.

COMPLETED INSULATION LAYER
Awaiting finish plaster. Note the massive foundation. This oven was built in New York state, where flagstone is abundant.

LAYERS OF STRAW-CLAY, & FINISH PLASTERING

Applying straw-clay to an oven, without a frame in which to compact it, poses a challenge: how to make it dense enough to be fireproof? The answer is to add extra clay to the layer nearest the fire. While it will diminish the insulation value, too little clay and the straw will burn, or at least smolder and char. Use less clay as you move farther away from the heat source. You'll always want enough clay on the straw to make it sticky. When you go to plaster it, don't worry if the insulation seems soft and squishy; push the plaster into it. It will dry firm and solid. If it doesn't add another layer.

MAKING A REINFORCED DOOR FRAME

Because straw-clay won't make a durable or flame-resistant doorframe, you need to make one of cob extending out from the actual oven dome like the doorway to an igloo. It should be as wide as the thickness of your insulation, and of material dry enough to support itself. (If the mix doesn't seem to stick, wet it a bit, add clay, or paint the joint with a thin glue of clay and water.) Make thick ropes or "straps" of cob, and mold the frame with those. Start at the bottom on either side of the hearth tongue with an angled wedge of cob. Work your way up in layers, keeping the edges clean as you go, and extending the layers toward the center, until they meet over the top of the doorway. They will make a ledge that you can build onto, including a chimney (the cob may need to dry before it will support a chimney). When your doorway is finished, you're ready for straw clay.

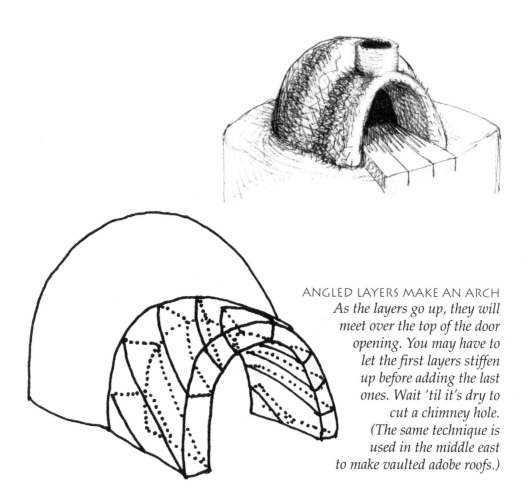

ANGLED LAYERS MAKE AN ARCH
As the layers go up, they will meet over the top of the door opening. You may have to let the first layers stiffen up before adding the last ones. Wait 'til it's dry to cut a chimney hole. (The same technique is used in the middle east to make vaulted adobe roofs.)

EXPERIMENTS & THINGS TO TRY

There are lots of intriguing ideas that I haven't had a chance to try out or research further. You may want to do your own research and/or find expert advice before you test them. If you have interesting results and want to share, let me know and I'll try to include them in a future edition.

GLAZING INTERIOR
OVEN SURFACES WITH SALT OR BORAX

Potters have long used a variety of salts (including regular table salt) to glaze pottery. They introduce the salt into a hot kiln, where it vaporizes and fuses with compounds in the clay, producing a hard, glassy surface. Ovens don't normally get as hot as kilns, but I have heard of people using salt in a similar way. Perhaps the lower heat of the oven is actually an advantage, allowing the salt to harden the clay without creating a rigid coating that could crack and spall? One potter suggested that borax, which fluxes at lower temperatures, might be a better option for bread ovens. He also warned that burning salt at high temperatures creates toxic fumes that can be harmful to plants, humans, and other animals.

TEXTURED SURFACES TO IMPROVE HEAT TRANSFER

Since increased surface area increases the rate of heat transfer, it seems reasonable to think that a textured dome would make a more effective oven. Here are some ideas:

- Carve ridges into an existing dome (easier in a big oven).
- Make a clay-reinforced form, carve ridges into it, and mold the oven over them. Remove the form and the ridges remain.
- Press small chunks of wood into the sand form, and pack cob tight around them. They'll fall or burn out, leaving a textured surface. Size and space them to avoid creating thin spots that might break off and drop onto the bread.
- Press rocks into the sand form so that they become imbedded in the oven dome — maybe red "lava rocks" like the ones used for gas barbecues? Size and space them as above. See how various materials work together.
- As this book was going to press, I heard about an Iraqi baker who remembers flat-bread ovens with pebble floors (what kind of pebble would be a crucial piece of information, since some rock explodes in high heat). Flat bread was tossed directly on, creating a dimpled effect now duplicated with fingertips. Customers were apparently responsible for removing the occasional pebble. The baker tossed in new pebbles as needed.

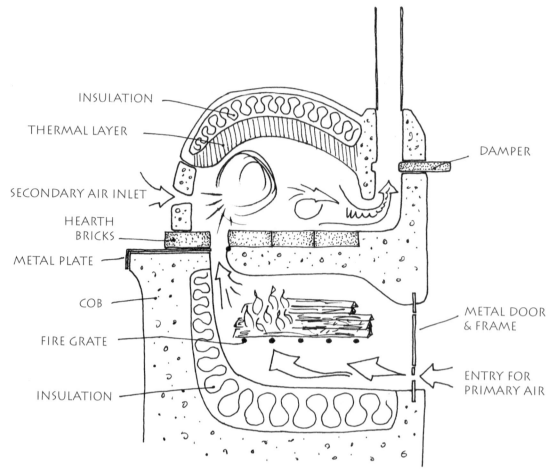

INSULATION

THERMAL LAYER

DAMPER

SECONDARY AIR INLET

HEARTH BRICKS

METAL PLATE

COB

FIRE GRATE

INSULATION

METAL DOOR & FRAME

ENTRY FOR PRIMARY AIR

THE HEARTH BRICKS SLIDE ON THE METAL PLATE TO SEAL THE OVEN DURING BAKING.

TWO-CHAMBER OVENS

My latest home oven is a two-chamber design with a separate fire box below the oven chamber. The idea is that the oven becomes a "secondary burn chamber," where fresh air helps ignite unburned gases. The goal is to get more heat from the same fuel, a cleaner, more efficient oven, and a clean, "no scuffle" baking surface. I have seen such designs described in various places, and inspected one in England, but the jury is still out on mine. I've baked in it a couple of times and burnt a lot of wood, but it's still drying out after a winter with no roof. In addition, I'm not sure my clay soil will stand up to the higher temperatures that it generates. It might require higher quality clay, refractory cement, or brick. Design and construction required more thought towards flues and dampers, doors, controlling draft, insulating the fire box (to avoid losing heat to nonessential areas of the oven), etc.

PIZZA
OVEN TO GO:
I was invited to make a temporary pizza oven for a summer festival, but I decided that mobile was better than temporary, even though I wasn't sure how to do it. The oven box is suspended on motorcycle shocks (lower R.), a solution inspired by Hannah, and designed and built by a welder friend, in a lot more time than it took to build the oven! Hannah was head baker, and made 500 pizzas in two days. (Ann Wiseman bottom photo)

OVENS THAT HEAT YOUR HOME AS WELL AS BAKE, OR FURNACES THAT BAKE

If you go so far as to build a two-chambered oven, you might as well heat your home too. That's the idea of the Finnish fireplace, Russian flue, or masonry heater — a furnace that burns very hot, very fast, but soaks up almost all the heat of the fire through a complex venting system contained within a very dense, heavy masonry shell. Many designs include bread ovens. Building one is a major project involving much more technical masonry than a mud oven, but books and workshops are available. See Resources.

WHY SMOKE?

A clean, efficient wood fire produces energy (heat), carbon dioxide (a harmless gas), water, and trace minerals (ash). A dirty, inefficient fire creates energy, carbon monoxide (poisonous and flammable), water, ash, and unburned fuel in the form of smoke and soot. That is why you get smoke before fire — because the reaction hasn't heated up enough yet to burn hot and clean.

CHAPTER SIX: PYRODYNAMICS, OR, PLAYING WITH FIRE

MECHANICS OF FIRE

Burning, or "oxidation," is happening most of the time to most materials on the planet (more about that later). So when you touch a match to something flammable, all you are doing is adding heat to an already ongoing reaction between fuel and oxygen. The match adds enough extra energy to the reaction to speed it up to the point where it creates more heat than it uses. The breaking of chemical bonds releases enough new energy to break even more bonds. With adequate fuel and oxygen, and nothing to cool it down, the reaction grows.

Complete combustion requires thorough mixing of fuel and oxygen. The fuel must not only ignite, but burn completely before it goes up the chimney or out the door. Smoke is a clear sign that you have incomplete combustion, because smoke contains unburned particles and gases. Smoke is unavoidable, at least in your oven, but you *can* minimize it.

The most efficient oven, in terms of fire, is the one that bakes the most bread with the least fuel. Retained heat ovens may not make the best sense where fuel is scarce, but there are places where a narrow definition of efficiency can't and shouldn't be the main criterion for building ovens. Where fuel is abundant and/or easily renewed, wood-fired, retained heat ovens may make much more sense than coal, oil, or nuclear (electric) powered ovens — especially if they are well-insulated and kept in continuous use.

So it is worth paying attention to how your fire burns, and learning how to achieve the highest, best use of what is, after all, a very precious thing — the heat of the sun as stored in a chunk of a once-living tree. How your fire burns is primarily controlled by three variables: time, temperature, and turbulence. Rubbing two sticks together the old-fashioned way illustrates the relationship between time and temperature: they will only burn when friction and pressure have raised the temperature to the point of ignition. But you've already speeded things up by putting a match to paper, kindling, and good dry wood. You can't do much more with time and temperature.

So you're left to work with turbulence — the mixing up of your burning fuel with the hot air (oxygen) that it needs to burn. What do you do when you've rubbed your two sticks

AN EFFICIENT RESOURCE
If you need to answer questions of fuel efficiency, conservation, pollution, and ethics before you build an oven, one place to start might be articles about oven efficiency by John Selker and Eric Shirey, who studied the issue in so-called "Third World" countries (in Cookstove News, reprints available from Ovencrafters in California).

long enough to make smoke and a little fire? You blow on it; not so hard that you reduce the temperature below the burning point, but hard enough to increase available oxygen and stir it all up.

You can increase turbulence in your oven the same way by using a bellows to blow a fast stream of air into the fire. Or you can take advantage of the draft produced by a rising column of warm air, as in a chimney. If you watch a fire in a chimneyless oven, you'll see that the smoke spills out the top half of the door while the air flows in through the bottom half. So it makes sense that there should be a relationship between the size of the chimney and the size of the door.

Adding a chimney and reducing the opening through which air reaches the fire creates a Venturi effect. The Venturi effect is what happens in a garden hose with a small nozzle: when you force the same amount of water through a smaller hole, it comes out faster and at higher pressure. The same applies to air: the smaller the opening, the faster the flow. In a hose, however, pressure *pushes* the water *out*. In an oven, the chimney *pulls* air *in* — so to increase the effect, you reduce the size of the door opening, *not* the size of the chimney.

This effect is how people created the first kilns — basically, big mud ovens with high chimneys, very strong draft, and carefully designed doors. For a bread oven, however, you're less interested in high temperatures (kilns are fired to more than 2,000 degrees Fahrenheit) than in thoroughly heating the mass of the whole oven to a temperature adequate for baking. This is a matter of heat transfer, not combustion — how to move heat from the fire into the mass of the oven. At its simplest, it's a matter of getting a hot, bright fire as quickly as possible. Watch, and adjust as needed.

Sometimes, even without a chimney, partially blocking the doorway can give you a much brighter fire with less smoke — an improvement. When an oven with a front chimney seemed to be burning poorly, friend Jason suggested punching a small hole in the back, opposite the door, to improve airflow. It helped. So it's worth experimenting. And if it doesn't work, you can always mud it over.

SOME RELATED PRINCIPLES

The simple addition of chimney and outer door increases not only turbulence, but also temperature and the amount of time that fuel and oxygen have for mixing. By tinkering with various ovens, I've gained an appreciation for various kiln and stove design principles that others have figured out over the years. Tinkering will certainly teach you what works best for your oven, but first principles are worth considering:

Heat transfer in a given material is a constant — like top speed for a car. Clay can hold lots of heat, but it can absorb it only so much at a time. Different materials, with different densities and molecular structure, have different rates of heat transfer — heat moves through metal much faster than it does through clay. By the same token, however, metal doesn't hold heat as long. Given the same amount of heat over the same time, a cast iron oven would heat up *and* cool off faster than a clay oven.

Given an earth oven, all you can really do is optimize the combination of time and temperature (the duration of the fire, and its intensity). For instance, while a welding torch might give you 1,000 degrees more heat than a wood fire, the masonry wouldn't be able to absorb it — the extra heat would go up the chimney. On the other hand, if your fire is too small and too slow, the heat will also be lost because it will have time to pass completely through the oven.

You can increase the rate of heat transfer by increasing surface area. Think of a sailboat. The bigger the sail, the faster it goes. The greater the surface area of the oven, the more heat it can "catch." But you don't want a bigger oven, because it would take more material and require even more heat. So increase the *texture* of the oven surface, like folding a sheet of paper into a fan. An oven with a highly textured inner surface — like a waffle, or corrugated cardboard — can increase efficiency.

A few other principles are worth mentioning in a general way, as they govern the larger forces that make it possible for kiln and stove designers to achieve desired effects for various purposes, from home-heating, to bread, to ceramics:

PRESSURE: Air, like water, has weight, and weight creates pressure. (An increase in pressure is what makes your ears "pop" in the deep end of the pool or on a drive up a mountain road.) Pressure increases as you go down because there's more weight above you. In other words, air at sea level is heavier than mountain air — that weight creates pressure, which makes air (or water) move.

TEMPERATURE affects pressure. That's why car tires say "inflate when cold." In warm air, molecules move faster. If they can spread out, the same volume of air will contain fewer molecules, weigh less, and rise. If they're trapped in a closed space like a tire, their movement creates an increase in pressure. Pockets of air rise and fall as they gain and lose heat, creating currents, drafty houses, and on a large scale, weather.

DRAFT is an upward current of air created when buoyant light air draws heavier air upwards (also called the chimney effect). Warmer air is more buoyant, so it moves farther, faster. When you enclose a column of air in an actual chimney, you effectively concentrate the draft effect into a smaller area, increasing the...

RATE OF DRAFT: Increase the height of the chimney and the rate of draft increases. Taper it, and you increase draft even further (because you've reduced the amount of stuff in the column, thus reducing the weight of air above, and the atmospheric pressure below). Rate of draft determines how much oxygen the chimney pulls into the fire, which in turn affects how it burns.

RESOURCE
Ovens are similar in history and design to early kilns used for firing ceramics. These principles are drawn from The Bread Builders, by Dan Wing and Alan Scott, pp. 198-200; and the chapter on "Principles of Kiln Design," in The Kiln Book, by Frederick L. Olsen.

In kiln design, specific ratios determine how much chimney height is needed to "pull" air through a chamber of a given size. One kiln designer suggests three feet of chimney height for every vertical foot of "pull," and one foot of chimney height for every unit of horizontal "pull." ("Pull" is the distance that air will have to travel before it can enter the chimney.) A home bread oven is small enough that this will be a minor consideration, but it's worth keeping in mind that a downdraft design will have a shorter "pull" than a crossdraft, and so probably needs less chimney height.

THE METAPHYSICS OF FIRE

In biology, there are two fundamental equations: the equation of burning and the equation of photosynthesis. Photosynthesis is how energy, carbon dioxide, water, and minerals combine to become the living flesh of plants. The energy is sunlight, and the minerals are soil. Combined with carbon dioxide and water, they are life.

But what about those who can't digest pure sun, rain, air, and earth? They rely on the equation of burning. Everything living burns. This is only partly oversimplification, because burning is fundamentally a chemical reaction between oxygen and the rest of the world, living or not. Even metal burns at a high enough temperature, and at low temperatures it reacts with oxygen and rusts, or "oxidizes," which is a very slow form of burning.

Back in the realm of the living, when oxygen reacts with carbon and hydrogen, it produces carbon dioxide, water, and energy (usually in the form of heat and/or light). We don't all spontaneously combust because burning happens at different rates. The intensity of burning can be just enough to keep your body at 98.6 degrees, or it can be enough to heat an oven to 700 degrees. The variables have to do with fuel and the speed of the reaction. The burning of a wood fire is different than the burning of sugars to make muscular and nervous energy, to move your arms and legs, to grab a carton of milk in the supermarket — and that is different than the (explosive!) burning of fossil fuel in your car engine as you drive home to deliver the carton of milk to your kitchen table. But basically, all fuels are some combination of carbon and hydrogen — which makes sense, since "fossil fuels" are, after all, the fossilized bodies of once living plants.

What's all this got to do with ovens and bread? Well, everything! The history of our race (indeed, the planet) begins and ends with the same question: What, when, where, why and how do we burn? Call it magic, science, or religion (remember Moses and the burning bush?) — burning is an extraordinary fact of life. But it's easy to ignore among the endless details of modern human busy-ness. Which is a whole 'nother kind of burning. So remember that when we eat bread, we absorb the sun that grew the grain, and the sun that grew the trees. The fire in your oven and the fire in your belly are the same marvelous thing. Tend them carefully, and be grateful.

RESOURCE
Much of this information was drawn from William Bryant Logan's Dirt, The Ecstatic Skin of the Earth, *and Harold McGee's "Chemistry Primer" in* On Food and Cooking.

"FROBEARILLA," OREGON, 1999
Built by 6 young men as part of a "arts-in-education" project in a foster home. They also worked with a writer to record and reflect on their experience in prose and verse.

CHAPTER SEVEN: TROUBLESHOOTING

MY SAND FORM WON'T HOLD ITS SHAPE

Several things make sand so generally moldable. Water provides a weak electrical "glue." The facets and edges of many different sized particles provide friction and a tendency to interlock. In general, the more edges and facets on each grain, the better they hold together. The size of the grains, and having a mix of sizes, are both also important. All this is very important in the building of roads, where the ability of aggregates to "lock" together can wreck or save the maintenance budget. So — try the following (in order of simplest to most involved):

Add water. If that doesn't help, and your sand seems very coarse, with few small grains to fill the spaces between large grains, try adding *a bit* of clay (no more than half of what you would put in a building mix). If your sand is very wet, even the addition of dry clay can make it go more liquid; so mix your clay with fresh, dry sand, if possible. If not, you may have to let it dry out.

I HAVE NO SAND — HOW ELSE CAN I MAKE A FORM?

Topsoil will make a fine form (though it's a bit harder to dig out — don't forget to use a parting layer of wet newspaper). You could try making a dome of straw tied with twine! Whatever you have will suggest its own solution.

There are also alternatives to a solid form of sand, though I don't think any of them are better or simpler. Canadian style ovens are made on a "basket" made of bent, tied saplings that burn out upon firing. You can mold a dome of chicken wire. One woman wrote me that she tried a frame of garden lattice, and when that didn't work, tried a cardboard packing tube. Anything might do, but remember that if it can absorb water (like a cardboard tube), it will lose strength and might collapse before you're ready.

I CAN'T FIND STRAW

Straw isn't strictly necessary. Your oven will work fine without it. Straw helps bind mud together, especially when wet. In large enough quantities, and mixed with a minimal amount of clay, it also insulates.

If you're looking for insulating material, coarse sawdust mixed with clay will also insulate. The best materials for insulation are rock products that will cost money, but if you're making a serious oven, of if you absolutely can't find anything else, it's worth spending the dough on perlite, vermiculite, or pumice. (See Chapter Five on "Insulating a mud oven.")

MY FIRE WON'T BURN

Wait. See if it doesn't burn better as the fire moves back into the oven. Play with it. You may have overloaded your oven with too much fuel, and blocked the airflow — open a passage for air to reach the back, or remove some fuel. Review the chapter on fire. Your door may be too low; try carving it back so it's a bit higher. Your fuel may be wet. Dry it out.

The wind can interfere with how a fire burns — see Chapter Five on chimneys and doors; place some bricks around the oven door to shield it from blowing air, and see how the fire responds.

THE BOTTOMS OF MY LOAVES ALWAYS BURN

Try soaking the oven longer before you bake.

Build your fire on a bed of ashes from the previous fire; this will help insulate the floor against excessive heat buildup.

If your bread has to go in the oven NOW and there's NO time to soak the oven and flour practically EXPLODES in flame when you toss some on the floor, try baking on cookie sheets turned upside down; or use a soaking wet scuffle/mop and repeated swabbings to cool off the floor (but be warned that this will shorten the life of any floor).

MY OVEN IS CRACKING

Some cracking is inevitable. Most will not be a cause for concern. All clays shrink as they dry; some more, some less. Adding sand to your mix can minimize this effect. Ovens develop cracks during firing due to the natural expansion and contraction caused by tremendous changes in temperature. Cracks that don't close up can be filled with fresh material (from the outside), or not. I've baked in cracked ovens with no problem.

If your oven is literally falling apart, your material may have lacked clay. There may be nothing for it but to rebuild with better materials.

There are no materials that heat won't eventually damage or destroy. Even the finest firebrick cracks and wears out eventually.

GUAJOLOTE (TURKEY) OVEN, ATLANGA, MEXICO, 1996. *Fifty children helped build this oven in a community center three hours from Mexico City. The project was part of an environmental education program. The oven is supported by a cinder block arch, which also creates space for wood storage. Smoke vents out the back through a chimney made of cob over tin cans (buried in the head and neck); feet are cement for durability. (B. Steen photo)*

Air-drying may reduce cracking. Some shrinkage cracking will be unavoidable, as a result of the oven walls being effectively fixed to the oven floor, where they can't move. If you do air-dry, cover the oven with a heavy cloth to keep sun and moving air from speed-drying the surface, which would cause even more cracking (because the surface would be drying faster than the insides).

However you dry your oven, removing your sand form will help ease shrinkage cracking. Just be sure the oven is dry enough to hold up.

CAN I QUICK DRY MY OVEN?
(IN OTHER WORDS, WHEN CAN I LIGHT A FIRE?)

I have built and fire-dried ovens on the same day with no problem. They invariably shrink and crack, but most cracks are small. Really big ones (1/2 inch or more) can be filled (from the outside) with wet clay.

CAN I MAKE AN ALL-CLAY MIX THAT SHRINKS LESS?

When potters want to minimize shrinkage, they mix their clay with a product called "grog," which is fired, crushed clay. It works as a coarse aggregate, like sand, except that its expansion and contraction rates should be closer to that of your clay, thus reducing risk of gritty grains "popping" out. You can buy grog at a ceramics supply house, or make it by crushing up old brick. Think of it as sand, and try some test mixes to see what proportions work best with your clay.

THE DOORWAY IS CRUMBLING & FALLING APART

It's easy to rebuild a doorway with fresh cob, but if that doesn't work, see Chapter Four for ideas on brick and metal doorways.

I CAN'T FIND CLAY SUBSOIL ANYWHERE

You can build with silty, low-clay soils, but it will likely be weaker, softer, and more susceptible to damage. Also see Chapter Four on where else to find clay.

WHAT ELSE CAN I USE FOR FUEL BESIDES WOOD?

Gas (natural or propane) is probably the cheapest, most practical alternative to wood, but I've never tried it, so I can't offer much in the way of advice. But before you look for gas burners to adapt for oven use, look for sources of scrap wood. Cabinet- and furniture-makers often throw it away. Building contractors pay to have huge containers of wood hauled off site and dumped in an already over-full landfill. City and county road departments, arborists, and landscapers all produce lots of "waste" wood you might be able to collect. Prune your hedges and see if you don't get a baking's worth of wood! Green wood will need to air dry at least several months, or hurried up in a warm (not hot) oven.

ATHENA'S OWL, ARIZONA, 1996 A DESIGN THAT DIDN'T WORK *The consequence of sacrificing practicality for aesthetics is* frustration. *The bird's beak was meant to vent smoke through the nostrils, but they are clearly too small, and provided no advantage in terms of extra draft. The mistake could have been ameliorated with a higher door, or different chimney design. (B. Steen Photo)*

"GOONA ZOONA," NEW YORK, 1995

Another good reason to make the outside of your oven beautiful (or interesting, at least): it helps take your mind off your mistakes. I had some good advice, but got it backwards, and tried slanting the floor so it rose up to the back, away *from the chimney (the advice assumed the chimney was in the* rear). *As a result, at first, it burned poorly, but my brother later fixed it by installing a rear chimney.*

BUILD YOUR OWN EARTH OVEN

AFTERWORD

ART, EARTH, OVENS

I grew up with my mother, an artist and single parent who always had interesting projects at home, taught me to make bread, let me skip school a day a week in sixth grade to learn ceramics from an expert, and encouraged me to go to Italy at 17 to carve marble. So bread and art have been constants, but I only started to make my living at them a few years ago, after abandoning institutional employment (for the last time, I hope) for better bread, more sculpture, and less money. I didn't know exactly how I was going to go about it, but at one point, a friend who teaches anthropology invited me to hear a guest lecturer. She told me that he "lived on $3,000 a year in a mud house he'd built for $500." Given my prospects, I figured it might be useful.

The lecturer was a Welshman named Ianto Evans. He has lived and worked all over the world and gives slide lectures illustrating what is sometimes called "permaculture," or "appropriate technology." What I saw, however, was a brilliant and very specific illustration of the practical relationship between beauty and function — in everything from gardens to houses to stacks of brooms packed and loaded onto overloaded buses in Guatemala.

Ianto spent the night at a neighbor's house, so I got to visit and hear more about the "Cob Cottage Company," which he had just set up, with his wife, Linda Smiley, and another partner, Michael Smith. (Ianto's cob cottage is the one in the photo on page nine.) Cob Co. was offering hands-on courses on earthen building. I spent a week with them and about 15 other students, working on a small house. One afternoon, we built a mud oven similar to ovens made all over the world by all kinds of people. The next day we had fresh bread.

The next few months I spent traveling. When I arrived in Minnesota to visit my father and his wife of 30 years (my second mother), the highlight of every meal was Mary's bread, an absolutely wonderful, traditional European sourdough the likes of which I hadn't tasted since the summer I spent in France when I was 12. Mary's bread book recommended a "backyard brick oven." I suggested mud instead, and spent several hot, sticky Minnesota summer days digging a deep hole and converting an old section of limestone wall into a deep foundation (protection against the long, hard Minnesota winters — the frost line was two or three feet down). I dug and hauled sand and dirt by pickup truck and wheelbarrow, and finished the oven in another day or two. A few weeks later, when I got to my brother's house, I showed him pictures. Then he wanted one. Neighborhood kids helped, and it came out in the shape of a mythical creature. A three-year old named it "Goona Zoona."

Both ovens had some serious mistakes. My father convinced me to try a cement stucco on the first — it survives, but not in great shape. On the second one, my sister-in-law's brother suggested slanting the floor up towards the rear, to improve combustion. Which would have worked fine, if we'd built the chimney in back — but with a chimney in front, the fire couldn't burn all the way back — so my brother had to add a rear chimney. I tried a gypsum plaster on this one (no time to build a roof, and I didn't know about lime plasters), which may have soaked up more water than it shed. But the next summer, for my brother's wedding, I fired it up and baked three sourdough batches of about six loaves each. The first took 20 minutes, the second 45, and the third about an hour — with a single firing. When the old maple tree dropped a limb that winter, Goona Zoona took the blow. The next one will be better.

As for bread, I grew up watching my mother bake. She is an artist, and rarely uses recipes when she cooks. In a book she wrote on bread sculpture she said, "there are no mistakes, just new ways to make bread." She also helped me gain an appreciation for real bread by sending me to a farm in Brittany when I was 12 (an experience worth more than most camps). I learned French, worked in the fields, and got to know a bunch of French kids. I also ate lots of "pain de campagne." Once or twice a week, the grandmother bought several two- or three-foot loaves at the local bakery, and stored them in a big wooden box in the kitchen. Afternoon snack, or "goutée," was a thick slab, buttered and sprinkled with sugar. Breakfast was the same buttered slabs dipped in a bowl of hot milk, chocolate, or coffee. It was thick, chewy, and a little tart, with a strong brown crust that felt good between your teeth. Every time I dip toast in coffee, I remember that breakfast, and particularly that bread. But for too long it was a wistful memory, since such bread seemingly wasn't to be found or made on this side of the Atlantic.

Luckily, when I was learning to make ovens, my second mother was learning to make authentic French "pain au levain" (bread from starter). She also is an artist, but very precise and methodical, which is what production pottery

SNAIL OVEN, PHILO, CALIFORNIA, 1996
An excellent mason supervised the construction of this foundation of local river rock. When we discovered that the snail's shell spiralled in the wrong direction, we concluded that it must be an "anti-snail" to protect the garden. It was built as part of a Natural Building Colloquium next to a hybrid, straw-bale and cob greenhouse.

requires in order to make a living at it. Not surprisingly, she makes good use of cookbooks, where she learned to make traditional sourdoughs.

I later bought the book and read it, but learned most by watching Mary tend her jars of wild yeast starters and knead her dough for 15 minutes by the clock. While I had made decent bread for years, seeing Mary at work helped me understand why her bread was so good. And as my own bread improved, I was also making ovens, and noticing the small but significant ways in which bread was consistently better out of a mud oven. It took a little while for my brain to catch up with what my body was doing, but I finally made the "aha!" connection between dough and oven.

While I have made some pretty nice loaves in a modern range, modern baking (and much of modern life) knows very little about that practical, beautiful, and essential phenomenon that transforms earth, water, air, and fire into life. The bread cycle begins with fertile soil, sun, and seed, and gives us grain and flour and loaf and life. It is an impressive debt we take on; one we can only repay, in the end, with our lives and our bodies. Dust we are, and to dust we return. But it's holy dust, and like the phoenix, it will be reborn in the next turn of the cycle.

Like all art and craft, oven-building and bread-baking heighten your awareness of that essential cycle of bread and life — things that are, in the end, beyond understanding. Whether or not you understand all the hows and whys doesn't really matter. If you make bread, *you can make bread!* What is important and valuable is that you do it — and not just because good artisan loaves fetch outrageous prices in the fancy markets.

The real value of good bread, I think, may be this: when you are aware of your relationships with the world, you realize they can't be measured on a modern monetary scale. Real value is a function of involvement and life. We are told in so many ways that life is about earning and spending money that we tend to think of our time the same way. But money is just a means of exchange, and not a value.

Romanian sculptor Constantin Brancusi said that "sculpture must be lovely to touch, friendly to live with, not only well-made." If that doesn't describe bread, I will stop eating. Bread, like art, is an invitation — to sit, to rest, to tell stories; to cook, to share, to make parties, feasts, and festivals. Making an earthen oven is also such an invitation, and its full, round form is indeed, "lovely to touch, friendly to live with...." And while

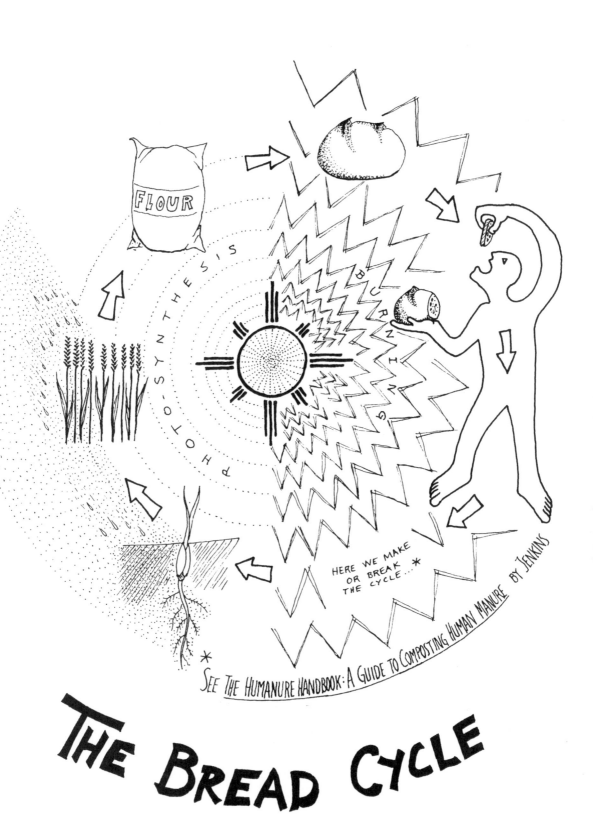

FLOUR

PHOTO-SYNTHESIS

BURNING

HERE WE MAKE
OR BREAK
THE CYCLE... *

* SEE THE HUMANURE HANDBOOK: A GUIDE TO COMPOSTING HUMAN MANURE BY JENKINS

THE BREAD CYCLE

BREAD & FREEDOM
I recently went to a panel discussion about the 1999 World Trade Organization meeting in Seattle. I heard about European citizens who didn't want to eat beef treated with hormones. The WTO allowed the US to punish them with trade sanctions until they lifted their ban on our beef. That didn't sound free to me. I don't want to eat hormone-treated beef either. But the WTO gives that kind of power to corporate business. The conflict reminds me of David and Goliath, taxation without representation, all the issues for which America fought the revolutionary war. Unelected kings aren't much different than unelected companies. And corporations aren't even people. They have all the rights of people, but much more money and so, more power. So I sat there thinking about what to say or do...., What came to my mind was: Grow a garden, buy organic flour, make bread.... Such is not protest, it is principle.

bread and ovens are rarely immortalized in museums and history books, they are art — they are the shaping of materials to create new forms and thus, new life. Some object that this is craft, not art. But it seems to me that trying to separate art from craft is like trying to isolate beauty from life. Art is not born in galleries — it is our common heritage, and if you can become completely absorbed, even for a moment, in the creation of something new — be it as simple as a mud oven or a loaf of bread — you know something that no one can teach and that no one can buy.

What's the alternative? If we are what we eat, then what do we become when we eat bread from factories where human hands never touch the dough? What relationships are we nurturing? Is corporate-sponsored consumerism our ultimate and final purpose?

Life doesn't ask us to buy, it asks us to participate — to watch, to learn, and to create. To be either artist or craftsman is no more and no less than it is to be human: to engage hands, head, and heart in the genesis of form and relationship; to celebrate and renew self and world; to be whole and wholly involved; to offer communion and to build community; or just to make a mud oven so you can bake your own bread.

MUD MAN, REPRISE, OREGON, 1999
Built in a workshop at a Methodist camp and retreat center. The oven is now protected by a lovely pole structure with a "living roof" of sod. The site is part of an "indigenous village" used by young campers in the summer.

APPENDIX: QUESTIONS, ANSWERS & RESOURCES

Since the first printing, various readers and workshop partici-
pants have asked good questions that warranted a few more
pages. If you can't find an answer to your question here or in
the main text (please be sure to try out the new index!), feel
free to contact me.

ABOUT EFFICIENCY, DESIGN, ETC.

Q: How efficient are earthen ovens?

A: There are two things to consider here. First, since you
      have to heat up the whole mass of a retained heat oven in
      order to bake, clearly, cooking just a few loaves of bread
      won't make efficient use of all your fuel. However, the
      more you cook, the more of the stored heat you use up,
      and the better your efficiency. Insulating an oven in-
      creases efficiency even more, as does using it again before
      it cools off (daily use, of course, is best). Alan Scott told
      me that one baker he knew cooked 630 pounds of dough
      with the heat from 130 pounds of wood (the oven was
      hot from the previous day). That was sixteen and a half
      bakes from a single firing! Better than 250 two pound
      loaves! That's almost 5 pounds of dough baked per
      pound of wood burnt — pretty good!
         Second, smoke is unburnt fuel, so a smoky fire is not
      efficient. If your oven is already hot, it will burn cleaner
      because the masonry won't be sucking heat out of the fire
      so fast. There are, also, many designs for wood-fired
      ovens. Some burn much cleaner and more efficiently than
      a cold earthen or masonry oven. However, you can make
      your mud-oven burn cleaner by using the driest wood;
      starting with a small fire, building it up slowly, and
      insulating. Or, if you only want to bake a couple of
      loaves, you can build a super-efficient oven that heats just
      air. (See the next question.)
         If you want a super efficient, clean fire *and* a retained
      heat oven, (and you live in a cold climate) you may want
      to build a traditional masonry heater, such as those
      described in *The Book of Masonry Stoves*. (See Resources,
      and the chapter on fire, p. 93.)

Q: I'm looking to build indoor masonry heater type units
      out of earth for heating and cooking. Any ideas?

A: The only published info I've seen on (part) earthen,
      masonry-style heaters/cookers is out of Aprovecho

Research Center (see Resources). Ask for "Capturing Heat," two slim volumes that also include simple designs for super-efficient ovens. Also ask the Cob Cottage Company about "Rocket Stove/Pyromania" workshops.

Q: Is there any effective difference between the Quebec shape and the beehive shape?
A: Interesting question. If you need a wide door (for pizzas or cookie trays) but don't want to hugely increase the diameter of your oven, or if you bake in square pans and want a longer shape with corners, a long oven can have a wider door without giving up so much of its thermal mass. That longer, egg-like shape is the major feature of the Quebec oven. If that suits your needs, then I'd say it's a better design for you. Some say it is more efficient, but I haven't seen or made any tests. Whichever design you use, try to make your dome no more than 16" high, since a big volume reduces the concentration of steam during baking, and that means your loaves won't get so nice and crusty.

Q: Have you experimented with electric heating elements?
A: One reader wrote that he had tried a 3000 watt range element in an oven made of refractory cement. He said it never got up to temperature, even after 8 hours. A nichrome kiln element might provide more heat. And, like a kiln, I imagine it would be good to place the element in a channel, to increase surface area and contact between the element and the oven material. But that's going to get complicated. Also consider that (in all cases except hydro- or solar power) electricity requires burning fuel to generate electricity to generate heat again – wasting large amounts of energy at every step – a very inefficient way to bake.

  I met a commercial baker who switched to propane when he got tired of splitting wood for his brick oven. But he said wood gave him a "deeper heat" – longer lasting and more effective.

Q: Is it better to build my oven with or without a chimney?
A: When I first wrote the book I thought chimneys made better ovens because they made a faster, hotter fire. Now I think the traditional oven with no chimney is probably best – if the smoke won't cause problems. If you need to control smoke, then yes, a chimney is best.

I changed my mind after experimenting with a cross-draft oven, which burned well, but used lots of wood. It illustrated a basic fact that I understood, but didn't quite accept; that is, no matter where you put it, a chimney sucks heat out of the fire. An oven without a chimney burns more slowly, giving the oven mass more time to absorb the heat of the fire.

USING THE OVEN

Q: I built a small oven that burns OK to start with, but no matter how I play with the fuel, it gets very smokey and goes out. The door is 63% of the interior height of the oven, so what am I doing wrong?

A: Since the cut of the doorway will tend to angle down, the inside edge of your door may be lower than the outside edge. So be sure to measure door height at the edge furthest inside the oven.

If your door is the right height, you've played with the fire (see p. 100), and the oven still won't burn, try cutting the door a bit higher, or making a hole through the back of the oven. Both provide more oxygen for combustion. The hole should be opposite the door, just above floor level, and at least as big as a quarter. (Plug it up with mud or a stick when you bake.)

And finally, the biggest combustion problems tend to be in the smallest ovens – which makes sense, since the smaller your oven, the lower the dome, and the less room for the fire to burn. A small oven should work, but might need smaller wood, closer tending, and longer burning.

Q: Do you find that cleaning the oven causes damage?

A: I'm pretty careful to keep the hard edges of my scuffle and peel away from the oven walls. It is harder, sometimes, to be so careful when tossing wood into a raging fire – but not impossible. I have noticed that ovens with a metal door support, or a pre-fabricated door and frame, tend to crumble where mud meets metal. I assume this is because hot metal expands more than hot clay. However, it doesn't seem to impair overall oven effectiveness.

Perhaps the greater risk is thermal shock, which can crack floor bricks and generally weaken oven materials. It comes of using too much water, either for steaming bread or for cleaning (or cooling) a hot oven floor.

If you're being careful with your tools and still having problems with interior oven damage, it may be that your original mix is weak – perhaps too silty, or too sandy. Rebuilding the oven may be your best solution.

Q: The snap-swivel on my scuffle keeps breaking – help!
A: I had the same problem, so I made a stronger swivel by wrapping a turn of stiff wire loosely around the end of a cotter pin or the end of a nail. The other end of the wire holds my rag, and the cotter pin or nail is secured thru a hole in the end of my wooden handle. It works great.

Q: My nice wooden baking door is getting terribly charred. Do I just have to keep making new ones?
A: I soak my door in a bucket of water while I'm firing the oven. That way it chars less, and adds a bit of steam.

BROOM HANDLE W/HOLE DRILLED THRU

STIFF WIRE

COTTER PIN*

RAG

(*A NAIL WITH A HEAD WILL ALSO SERVE)

MATERIALS & CONSTRUCTION

Q: I built an all-clay oven but it's crumbly, and falling apart. It was definitely clay, not silt. What did I do wrong, and can I fix it?
A: The mix may have been too dry, or not tamped hard enough, or both. Either would prevent the clay from cementing into a single, solid mass. You might be able to save it with an internal plaster (if you can reach — see safety note below), or by just brushing out the worst of the loose material — it still ought to work, if the floor bricks stay secure and the walls are thick enough (you can always add more thickness if needed).

Q: How do I know when it's time to pull out the sand form?
A: I find it easiest to build with a dry-ish mix (see p. 33-35). Then you can pull the form as soon as the first layer is done. However, if you can make a dent in the first layer with your finger, you should wait. Test the material again in a few days (or weeks, depending on weather and your mix). To let air circulate and aid drying, dig a narrow tunnel into the base of the form (if the sand collapses, stop!) When it seems ready, dig a shallow hole into the sand form to expose a fresh bit of the first layer. If it's still soft enough to dent when poked, wait!

If, when you do pull the sand form, part of the oven does collapse, stop and let things dry out. You may be able to patch it up with a sticky plaster (use lots of straw and clay). You may also need to poke sticks or nails into the hole to give the plaster something to hold onto. If it was a minor collapse, and your oven is pretty thick, it might not make any difference and you can just leave it.

SAFETY NOTE: If it's a big oven, and you do apply an internal plaster, *don't* put your arms and head in the oven without another person there to help in case of collapse. I've never heard of it happening, but I don't want to.

Q: What's a good plaster if humidity is a problem?

A: If, by "humidity," you mean moisture in the air, there's nothing to worry about; neither lime nor mud plasters tend to soak up (unprecipitated) atmospheric moisture. Lime plaster is not necessarily "better" than plain mud, and both kinds of plaster still need a roof.

Q: Once the oven is complete, is it best to wait until after it's been used for a bit before the finish plaster is applied?

A: Earthen plasters don't go through any chemical changes, so speed of drying has minimal effect – apply them when it suits you. If they don't stick, spray the oven with water, or make a wetter mix.

   A good lime plaster, on the other hand, is best applied when the oven is still moist all the way through. Lime plasters require water and time to effect the chemical reaction that makes them durable. Therefore, they are best kept damp (even covered) for a week or more. If you use lime plaster on a dry oven, soak it before you start. Best to use lime water (i.e., water that has had a bit of lime soaking in it to make it alkaline) to improve the bond. Lime is caustic – see cautionary note below.

Q: Is there a difference between mason's lime and agricultural lime? Where can I get mason's lime?

A: Agricultural lime will NOT substitute for mason's lime. Ag lime is powdered limestone, or calcium carbonate, ($CaCO_3$). Farmers use it to make soil less acid.

   Mason's, or "hydrated" lime, is limestone that has been cooked at very high heat (over 1500° F.), which drives off a carbon dioxide molecule (CO_2), to create CaO, or quicklime. With the addition of water, CaO turns to calcium hydroxide ($Ca(OH)_2$. So lime plaster, when exposed to air, goes through a chemical reaction by which the soft calcium hydroxide exchanges a molecule of water (H_2O) for one of carbon dioxide (CO_2), and reverts to limestone.

   Any masonry supplier should have mason's lime. Get it as fresh as possible, since, like cement, it "goes off," or starts turning back to limestone if left to sit too long.

   SAFETY NOTE: Mason's lime is caustic – read the bag, and use gloves, goggles, and respirator as suggested. The best lime plaster is made by slaking quicklime into lime putty which, as long as it is wet, won't turn back into limestone. But quicklime is hard to find, and slaking gives off immense heat; please do your homework, and be careful. See the Resources section and *Lime in Building*.

Q: Should I let the first layer dry before adding the next, so I can fill any cracks before adding the next layer?

A: If you're building an all clay oven, the answer is a definite yes. Pure clay shrinks a lot – I've had cracks as big as a half an inch. If you let it dry completely, it's easy to fill cracks from the outside before adding another layer.

If, on the other hand, you're building with a good sand-clay mix with minimal shrink (see p. 23), the advantages of letting the first layer dry are negligible.

Q: Would it be good to fire the first layer to harden it?

A: Firing the first layer won't make any difference to the second layer. If you take apart an old oven, you'll see that only about an inch of clay bisques, or gets hot enough to harden (it goes lighter and is no longer sticky when wet).

Q: What about cracks? Should I worry about them?

A: Probably not — in my experience, cracking is a common phenomenon, but generally not a problem. I don't claim to be an expert on high-temperature masonry, but I'll pass on a few things I've gleaned:

In general, any material that goes from 50-700°F and up in the course of a few hours is going to relieve the stress of thermal shock by cracking – more or less. The thicker the mass, the more likely the oven can absorb the stress without cracking. It may be that thicker material (and masonry of fired brick?) survives the stress of thermal shock by sustaining many micro-cracks, while thinner material sustains fewer, larger cracks. (See David Lyle's *Book of Masonry Stoves*).

I imagine some cracking is simply due to the fact that materials expand with heat. I have seen at least one large masonry oven where the front hearth bricks had been pushed out a full half inch farther in front than on the sides! Some masons address that problem by building expansion joints into the masonry surrounding their fireboxes — i.e., they leave a piece of cardboard between firebox bricks and the rest of the masonry — when it burns out, it leaves a gap. Alan Scott hangs the concrete floor slab on rebar and leaves a 3/4 inch gap all around it — partly to keep heat from being conducted away from the slab, but also partly as an expansion joint.

Cracks can be useful. Some bakers recognize baking temperatures by the width of their oven cracks. But cracking can cause problems too. They allow flammable soot and heat to escape from the oven, and the soot, or nearby flammables, can ignite. *The Bread Builders* talks about two bakers who barely missed severe fires, both partly due to oven cracks (p. 140). However, one of the operations was over-firing their oven, trying to get more out of it than it was designed for. And of course, fire is only a risk if flammables are too close to a hot oven.

Some commercial ovens insulate with loose, non-flammable material, like perlite or vermiculite, on the assumption that it will fill cracks, and prevent the escape of heat and soot.

Q: I made a brick arch doorway and the center brick came loose – what did I do wrong?

A: The bricks hold best if the inside corners are actually touching and if there's a joint at the top center, rather than a brick (apologies for the drawing). This allows the central wedge of mortar to serve as a "keystone." If your door ends up with a brick in the center, try to make sure that the narrow end of the gap is a bit smaller than the brick. Then knock off just enough of the corners of the brick so that it will wedge into place, and make a key-stone. If the gap is too wide, try turning the brick on edge, or orienting it longwise, and carving it into a keystone.

Q: I couldn't find any pumice to insulate under the oven floor. I got vermiculite instead, but it seems too soft and squishy to support much weight — any suggestions?

A: Compared to perlite and pumice, vermiculite *is* soft. If you use it under the floor of your oven, mix it with some clay slip (see p. 86) and let it set up hard before you build on it. As for pumice, another source might be a concrete block and/or brick manufacturer.

RESOURCES

GOOD BOOKS & INFO ON BREAD & OVENS

The Bread Builders: Hearth Loaves and Masonry Ovens, Dan Wing and Alan Scott, 1999, Chelsea Green. A wonderful resource that illuminates basic principles of both bread and ovens; includes excellent plans (from Alan Scott) for building a commercial-grade masonry oven, as well as extensive sources for everything from modular ovens, to flour and oven tools.

The Bread Ovens of Quebec, by Lise Boily, Jean Francois Blanchette, 1979, Canadian Center for Folk Culture Studies, Ottawa Canada K1A 0M8. Explores the history of traditional Canadian clay ovens as a social and technological phenomenon, explained by those who made and used them. Includes a photo essay on oven construction.

Ovencrafters, run by Alan Scott, master oven-builder, and coauthor of *The Bread Builders;* 5600 Marshall-Petaluma Road, Petaluma, CA 94952, phone and fax: 415-663-9010; also on the web. Sells *The Bread Builders,* the Quebec oven book, authentic cast-iron doors for clay ovens, baking pans, oven tools, grain mills, mixers, prefab ovens, thermocouples and meters, reprints of *Cookstove News,* and brick oven consultation.

On Food and Cooking: The Science and Lore of the Kitchen, by Harold McGee, 1984; NY, Fireside (Simon & Schuster); answers all your questions about the whys and hows, principles and chemistry of bread, water, yeast, eggs, milk, and (almost) everything else that goes on in the kitchen.

The Bread Book: A Natural, Whole-Grain Seed-to-Loaf Approach to Real Bread, by Thom Leonard, 1990; 17 Station Street, Brookline, MA; simple instructions for Flemish Desem bread; also how to grow and mill your own grain, as well as plans and instructions (from Alan Scott) for building a brick oven.

The Laurel's Kitchen Bread Book, A Guide to Whole Grain Bread Making, by Laurel Robertson, with Carol Flinders and Bronwen Godfrey, Random House, 1984; complete instructions for making Flemish Desem bread, and others.

The Book of Masonry Stoves, by David Lyle, Chelsea Green, 1984; Lyle wants to encourage "new attitudes toward wood burning in North America." He focuses on a European style stove that burns very hot, very clean, and that absorbs almost all the heat of the fire, releasing it slowly over many hours. Such stoves are more efficient, effective, and safer than the newest American metal stoves. The book includes an extensive history of wood-buring, oven mechanics, and technical details of stove building. Other sources include *Finnish Fireplaces: The Heart of the Home,* by Albert Barden & Heikki Hyytiainen, 1993, Helsinki, The Finnish Building Center, and the Masonry Heater Association (mha-net.org).

Capturing Heat, 2 booklets show how to make simple, efficient cooking/heating stoves, insulated "fireless cookers," solar ovens, etc., $8 each; Aprovecho Research Center, 80574 Hazelton Rd, Cottage Grove, OR 97424, 541-942-8198.

Building a Wood-Fired Oven for Bread and Pizza, by Tom Jaine, 1996, Prospect Books, Totnes, Devon, UK. Very good history of ovens through the ages, as well as brick oven instructions.

The Kiln Book, by Frederick L. Olsen, 1983, Chilton Book Co., Radnor, PA 19089. More technical info, higher temperatures.

GOOD BOOKS ON EARTH & BUILDING

The Cobber's Companion ($20 cash), and *Earth Building and the Cob Revival, a Reader* ($10 cash); add $2 to process a check or money order; The Cob Cottage Co., Box 123, Cottage Grove, OR, 97424, 541-942-2005. ask about earthen building courses.

The Cob Builder's Handbook, by Becky Bee, $19.95, plus $4 S&H, Groundworks, POB 381, Murphy OR 97533. Ask about earthen building workshops.

Spectacular Vernacular: The Adobe Traditions of West Africa, Jean Louis Bourgeois & Carollee Pelos, Aperture, 1996; text & photo survey of an inspirational tradition of earthen building.

A Pattern Language, by Christopher Alexander et al, Oxford U. Press, 1977; a very useful book for designing spaces.

Dirt, The Ecstatic Skin of the Earth, by William Bryant Logan, Riverhead Press, 1995. Inspiration and information.

The Humanure Handbook: A Guide to Composting Human Manure, by Joe Jenkins, Jenkins Publishing. How to simply and safely compost your own manure instead of flushing it.

Lime in Building, by Jane Schofield, Black Dog Press; "A Practical Guide" to the use of lime in plastering; available from **Taylor Publishing**, a good source for these and other building books; POB 6985, Eureka CA 95502; 1-888-441-1632; www.northcoast.com/~tms.

There are a growing number of permaculture and natural building resources out there — many of them are on the web. A good resource is *The Last Straw Journal,* HC 66 Box 119, Hillsboro NM 88042, 505-895-5400; www.strawhomes.com.

INDEX

page numbers for illustrations are in *italics*.
thanks to reader Kathleen Marie for donating her work to compile this index

BUILD YOUR OWN EARTH OVEN

THANK YOU

To all who are and aren't named here: thank you for your generosity, inspiration, and example — Alan Scott; Alejandra Caballero & Paco Gomez; Andrew Whitley; Ann Wiseman; Bill & Athena Steen; Bob Carlson; Carrie Mitchell & Bill Daley; Catherine Wanek & Pete Fust; Charlie Bremer; Clark Sanders; Connie Battaile; Dan Wing; Dawn Leslie; Earl Kimball; Hannah Field; Ianto Evans, Linda Smiley, Michael Smith, & other cobbers; Jason Saunders & Kim Barker; Peter & Mary Denzer; Piet Vermeer; Sandy Arbogast; Suzannah Doyle & Corvallis Unity; Tee Corinne & Bev Brown; and Tim and Sterling Grant and their families, who gave me room to make a home and a garden where I could plant a few new seeds (given by yet other friends), watch them grow, and learn. One gift opens the way for many others. Thanks again

ABOUT THE AUTHOR
Kiko Denzer is an artist and builder in earth, stone, plaster, clay, concrete, and wood. His work includes public installations, private commissions, community ovens, teaching, writing, making home and studio (above), and growing garlic. He and his wife live in Oregon's central coast range.

A GALLERY OF OVENS & STORIES SENT IN BY READERS AND OTHER OVEN FRIENDS

(Photos courtesy of the oven builders, unless otherwise noted.)

HAIDA SUN

The sun figure is a modern mud interpretation of a Haida god — on the other side, wrapped around the door opening, is Raven, who brought fire to the people in the days when Gods and people spoke to each other. The base is a piece of steel penstock from an old hydro-electric plant up the river, topped with a wooden pallet that's well-protected from the hot oven floor by plenty of insulation. It's a fair-weather oven that gets tarped over when the rains come in from the Pacific ocean. Built and sculpted by Dennis Kuklok, in the rain-shadow of Washington's Olympic Peninsula. Dennis is a permaculturist who works internationally, and is affiliated with Zopilote and the Cob Cottage Company. For info about natural building and permaculture workshops in the US and Mexico, contact Cob Co. at 541-942-2005, or on the web at www.deatech.com/cobcottage. K. Denzer photo.

NORWEGIAN MUD

"I met Kiko and Hannah at a workshop where they they built a small earthoven in a couple of hours. I was amazed at how easy it was. So when I came home, I built a foundation and got some buckets of mud. I had 3 kids round for the weekend and anybody who has had kids milling around like there is no tomorrow, knows that 4 channels on TV is not enough…. Just as things got out of hand, I produced the mud and found that the kids were most helpful.

I built an earthoven to learn to build with earth. I plan to build a cordwood masonry house on an organic farm here in Norway. And the only way forward is to start small, as with ovens. (If you would like to help me build a home without plastic, cement and so on, let me know… My name is Knut Caspari; my e-mail is: sjolberg@online.no)

In 2002 I published Kiko's book in Norwegian and got some funny feedback. One guy wanted to know what firm built earthovens, and was surprised when I suggested he do it himself…."

BASKET OVEN

The beautiful wicker basket form is burnt out with the first fire. But by building it over such a form, Bernard Graves (in photo) teaches many skills: weaving, earthen building, and how to manage woodlands to cultivate basket materials. Graves is a Waldorf educator who focuses on experiential learning, or learning by doing. As director of The Hiram Trust, his primary concern is to "foster the ethos of education for sustainability" — something that must be felt to be known and understood. Graves and the Trust can be reached at 01453-764-065, in Stroud, UK, or at www.anth.org.uk/hiramtrust. E. Holliday photo.

URBAN MUD

After helping build an oven at college, Beth Ferguson worked with an inner-city community organization in New York City's Bronx neighborhood, where she led more than 50 community members in building a cob oven for their community garden. All the materials were recycled or re-claimed from the urban "waste stream." The oven provides a central focus for the garden, and great food.

PIG IN THE GARDEN

The pig sculptors were part of a community youth garden program for "at-risk" kids (aren't we all?) They get paid to help grow and distribute organic produce to local shelters. Events and fund-raisers feature wood-fired pizza with garden produce. Desiré designed the pig. The foundation is cast concrete fence posts that were headed to the dump. Hannah Field and Tracy Noel led the project in Corvallis (Oregon). The kids later worked with a timber-framer to make a shelter, and are now working on a tile and flagstone mosaic path connecting the garden and oven. K. Denzer photo.

"OUR" OVEN

Sculpted oven & bench, part of a summer kitchen, built in workshops for OUR Ecovillage, Vancouver Island, BC. Elke Cole of Cobworks led the project. She is an architect who builds "houses that love you back;" and also teaches natural building; at least one past workshop included daily bread and desserts baked in a cob oven! Visit www.cobworks.com for programs and more info, or contact elke@cobworks.com, 250-539-5061.

VASHON TURTLE

Beautiful sculptural detailing, accented by blackberry dye on the shell, yellow ochre on the chest, and an oiled charcoal finish for the opening. The turtle, however, which was built for a workshop at a group house that already had an earthen oven, was later recycled "back into the pond." Builder Elias Adadow, of Vashon, WA, teaches oven and natural building, and can be reached at 360-331-7621.

FRIENDS, FIRE & DREAMS

"It was a community effort really, that included our Olympia Waldorf School 3d grade and other friends. The oven went up in 2 sessions separated by a week in between. The roof structure actually took a lot longer and was by far the most expensive part of the project. Actually, the cedar shingles were the only expense at roughly $60. We bake about once a week and often have guests young and old who want to participate in the process. In many ways this hearth has added a warm glow to the heart of our home. It's wonderful to have this fire presence activating friends and dreams."
— Warren Cohen, Olympia, WA

A PLAIN WORK OVEN

"A group of friends came over and we created the oven body in a day. It fires well, but the interior is a bit small, and we enlarged the door to handle our stew pots. Our family bakes 4 loaves of sourdough bread each weekend; before and after, we bake stew made of leftovers, a bit of venison, and garden vegtables. The base is local rock; the sand for the cement and the oven mix came out of the foundation hole."
— Sam Droege, Maryland

THE ENGLISH MUV'S OVEN

The base is a chunk of firewood saved from the axe, topped by a pallet, and insulated with straw and sawdust mixed with ample clay slip. The elegant dome roof is corrugated tin

attached to the pallet, bent over, and bolted at the top. The author and his (English) wife built it for their English Muv, Guli, prior to their wedding. Afterwards, it made great pizza for the guests. (Thanks Muv, for photos, and everything else!)

CANADA PUEBLO

Athena & Bill Steen, authors of *The Straw Bale House,* live and work in the Southwest, where earthen "hornos" are common, but they prefer the lower, longer shape of the Canadian style, as more efficient than the typical, high, round horno. Their work in natural building and the Canelo Project focuses on strengthening communities through strengthening self-sufficiency and participation. For info about oven and other building workshops, contact Joelee Joyce at DAWN / Out On Bale By Mail, in Tucson, AZ 85735, 520 624 1673, dawnaz@earthlink.net, www.greenbuilder.com/dawn.

KOOTENEY OVEN

Before they met, the author's wife, Hannah (not pictured), helped build this oven in the Kooteneys, of western Canada. It was made on a form of bent alder saplings, Canadian style. (Note the elegant ash dump.) During her time there, she read a newsletter article by an American oven builder who happened to live near some friends of hers in Oregon. Being a baker interested in wood-fired ovens, she decided to visit.... U. Holtkamp/S. Hennessey photo.

NINE ARGUMENTS FOR MUD

1. COMMUNITY

Just as the kitchen, or hearth, is the heart of a home, large communal ovens have long been the heart of communities. In the eighteenth century, after the Revolution that brought democracy to modern France, one of the first things the people did was to (re?) assert community control over the big ovens that had been under the regulation of feudal lords. According to Jerome Assire, in his *Book of Bread*,

> In rural Europe, the…various privileges [of the feudal system] included rights of banality over both mill and bakehouse, which were both the property of the suzerain. To bake their bread, the peasants were obliged to use these and these alone, and had to pay a duty to do so.

People wanted to reclaim what was naturally theirs: the right to make their own food, and the right to join hands so that heavy tasks could be made lighter for all.

From what I've seen of ovens built by folks with whom I've been in touch since writing this book, ovens and community still go together — whether community is the family, the neighborhood, a co-housing group, or a town with a new restaurant. And it isn't just the eating that joins us — it's the joy of mixing mud, getting dirty, having fun, and then finding, all of a sudden, that a *whole lot* of work has gotten done. Such shared labor can be a novel and pleasant surprise in this industrial culture where people often work alone in offices and facilities far removed from sun, soil, and neighbors.

2. The second, *and perhaps most important reason,* is that your kids can do it with you. Lots of people think that a wood-fired oven means that nothing but brick will do. But in addition to the cost (unless you're a mason and have trained your kids in the trade), it's unlikely they'll be able to help. However, as Knut Caspari found out in Norway, when you bring out the mud, all of a sudden, the kids can really help. And they may just learn something really important – not only the truth of "many hands making light work" – but also about the earth that gives them their food – especially critical info for young people who probably know more about computers than they do about

"With great pleasure you have inspired us greatly with your earth building imagination – thanks. Elliott (above) was the captain of the team. I took photos and video of our cob building adventure." — Jason Dix, owner of red barn ecofarm.

anything else. Mud is a way to find out for yourselves how it feels to be a plant, with roots that can follow water down into the fertile soil, and leaves that eat sunlight. Perhaps that's why it feels so good between the toes (and dough between the fingers)!?

3. Dirt is cheap. And if you still want a brick oven, mud is a good way to practice. You can make mistakes and learn *before* you spend hundreds (or thousands) on bricks and a mason. Start small: a 21" diameter floor area will bake several loaves, small pizzas, chickens, etc. and needs less wood and firing time. Our 31 by 23 inch home oven bakes a dozen 1.5 lbs loaves, and 3-4 hours of fire will bake two batches of bread, as well as casseroles, turkey, vegetables, soup, beans, etc. My biggest mud oven is at a restaurant: 4x4 foot on the inside; 9 foot diameter outside (see front pages for photo and story).

4. Mud *is* brick. Fire turns the inside of a "mud" oven to brick (quality varies w/soil, clay content, your mix, etc.).

5. Speed: I've built 12" diameter demo ovens in 15 minutes, and full-size ovens in half a day or less.

6. Custom design; you can make a fast-firing, thin-walled pizza oven, a big bread oven for a home business, a sculpted outdoor kitchen with seating, and more….

7. Sculptural freedom: you're not limited to rigid, rectilinear brick forms (not that I dislike rectangles…).

8. Temporal freedom: built right on the ground, or on planks and sawhorses, a quick oven can serve for a day or a year.

9. Carpenterial freedom: roofing not required: use a tarp (when the oven has cooled) or a piece of tin. (OK, so this isn't an advantage of mud per se, strictly speaking, but everyone always asks….)

A GALLERY OF OVENS

SPECIAL DISCOUNT:
20% OFF AND
FREE SHIPPING (US ONLY)
WITH THIS COUPON
...JUST $12 FOR A BOOK!

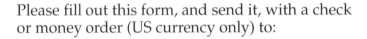

Please fill out this form, and send it, with a check or money order (US currency only) to:

Hand Print Press
POB 576
Blodgett, OR 97326
USA

name: _____

address: _____

city: _____

state: _____ zip: _____

telephone: _____

number ordered: _____ additional postage: _____
total: _____

For the 2d book, please add $3 shipping and handling, and one additional dollar for each additional copy.

Non-US customers: For postage to Canada please add $3; other countries, add $7. However, the book should also be available through bookstores or Amazon.com. If you do order here, please note that I can only accept a *postal* money order in US currency, or a check drawn on a US bank. I've also received many cash orders, and so far, none seem to have been lost — hurrah for the mail!

Call for bulk orders (5 or more) and bigger discounts
541-438-4300, or email: handiko@cmug.com